C++ Application Development with Code::Blocks

Develop advanced applications with Code::Blocks
quickly and efficiently with this concise, hands-on guide

Biplab Kumar Modak

BIRMINGHAM - MUMBAI

C++ Application Development with Code::Blocks

First published: October 2013

Production Reference: 1181013

Published by Packt Publishing Ltd.
Livery Place
35 Livery Street
Birmingham B3 2PB, UK.

ISBN 978-1-78328-341-5

www.packtpub.com

Cover Image by Paul Steven (mediakitchenuk@gmail.com)

Credits

Author
Biplab Kumar Modak

Reviewers
Zhia Chong

Lee Zhi Eng

Abhishek Gupta

Dinesh Subedi

Acquisition Editors
Sam Birch

Rebecca Youe

Commissioning Editor
Neil Alexander

Technical Editor
Dipika Gaonkar

Project Coordinator
Sageer Parkar

Proofreader
Ting Baker

Indexer
Hemangini Bari

Graphics
Sheetal Aute

Ronak Dhruv

Disha Haria

Production Coordinator
Aparna Bhagat

Cover Work
Aparna Bhagat

About the Author

Biplab Kumar Modak is a passionate, open-source software developer. He started learning programming at school in the year 1996 with a BBC Micro computer system. The sheer limitation of computing resources in a BBC Micro computer system forced him to think out-of-the-box and sharpened his programming skills. He participated in several software development competitions at school level and won several awards before joining college.

By then he started learning and developing in C and C++ language. He used his C/C++ development skills for his academic and extracurricular projects. He started contributing to the Code::Blocks project in the year 2006 and since then has remained as one of the developers of Code::Blocks. He has also contributed to a few other open source projects. Overall he has about 17 years of freelance software development experience and out of which 14 years in C/C++ development experience.

He is basically an Civil and Structural Engineer by profession. His job involves analyzing and designing tall buildings and other structures. He was one of the key engineers behind recent upgrade of Terminal 1, Singapore Changi Airport, and several public and private housing projects. He spends his free time in learning new technologies and in developing Code::Blocks and other such projects.

I want to thank Mr. Rabindra Prakash Sarkar for introducing me to the world of programming.

I also want to thank my parents for their support, encouragement, and blessings. I thank my wife, Ishita, for her support all these years. I would also like to thank Pampa, Pradip, Bubai, Shyamali Das and her family, Jibananda Mukherjee, all other family members, Atish, and my in-laws for their support and encouragement.

About the Reviewers

Zhia Chong is a young tech entrepreneur based in Seattle, WA. His background in technology ranges from C/C++ to Python. He recently graduated Magna Cum Laude from Gonzaga University with a Bachelor's degree in Computer Science and currently works for PaperG, a young startup in Seattle. He dedicates most of his time for writing beautiful, elegant code, and understanding business dynamics in the startup industry. He dreams of building his own successful startup.

He can be easily contacted via e-mail at zhiachong@gmail.com or his through website zhiachong.com.

Lee Zhi Eng is a 3D artist-turned-programmer. He has worked as a game artist and game programmer in several local game studios in his country; before becoming a contractor and a part-time lecturer at a local university, teaching game development subjects, in particularly related to Unity Engine, and Unreal Development Kit. You can find more information about him at http://www.zhieng.com.

Abhishek Gupta is a software engineer who has worked in the area of Automotive In-Vehicle Infotainment (IVI) since last two years. He has worked on a software-based HD video conferencing system as part of his MTech in Visual Information and Embedded Systems at IIT Kharagpur, India, in 2011.

He is passionate about video processing and loves to work on embedded multimedia systems.

Dinesh Subedi is a software developer at Yomari Incorporated Pvt. Ltd. He is currently working on data warehouse technology and business intelligence. He is a blogger at www.codeincodeblock.com. He writes writes articles related to software development using Code::Blocks IDE and has four years of experience in it.

He has completed a Bachelor's degree in Computer Engineering at Pulchowk Campus IOE Kathmandu, Nepal.

I would like to thank my friend Bibek Subedi and my brother Bharat Subedi who helped me while reviewing this book.

www.PacktPub.com

Support files, eBooks, discount offers and more

You might want to visit www.PacktPub.com for support files and downloads related to your book.

Did you know that Packt offers eBook versions of every book published, with PDF and ePub files available? You can upgrade to the eBook version at www.PacktPub.com and as a print book customer, you are entitled to a discount on the eBook copy. Get in touch with us at service@packtpub.com for more details.

At www.PacktPub.com, you can also read a collection of free technical articles, sign up for a range of free newsletters and receive exclusive discounts and offers on Packt books and eBooks.

http://PacktLib.PacktPub.com

Do you need instant solutions to your IT questions? PacktLib is Packt's online digital book library. Here, you can access, read and search across Packt's entire library of books.

Why Subscribe?
- Fully searchable across every book published by Packt
- Copy and paste, print and bookmark content
- On demand and accessible via web browser

Free Access for Packt account holders

If you have an account with Packt at www.PacktPub.com, you can use this to access PacktLib today and view nine entirely free books. Simply use your login credentials for immediate access.

Table of Contents

Preface

C++ Development with Code::Blocks is a concise and practical guide for application development using C++ and Code::Blocks. This book gives you several examples and step-by-step guides to begin with and then gradually progress to complex application development with C++. It also cleverly uses tutorials to elaborate Code::Blocks features for the readers. This book covers Code::Blocks Version 12.11. However, tutorials will be applicable to newer releases.

What this book covers

Chapter 1, Getting Started with Code::Blocks, will help us to install Code::Blocks on Windows and Linux.

Chapter 2, App Development with Code::Blocks, will help us to develop a simple app, to develop an app as a project, using external libraries with project, and concept of the workspace.

Chapter 3, App Debugging with Code::Blocks, explains the debugger related features offered by Code::Blocks and also to debug single and multiple apps.

Chapter 4, Windows App Development with Code::Blocks, describes how to develop apps using Code::Blocks for the Windows operating system. We will also learn to use wxWidgets and the way to use it for developing cross-platform apps.

Chapter 5, Programming Assignment, explains how to develop an app from scratch using Code::Blocks. We will look at a completed app, dissect it, and then develop it using Code::Blocks.

Appendix, discusses some advanced features of Code::Blocks. We will also learn about documentation generation, exporting source file, and so on in this chapter.

What you need for this book

The following software is required to learn and follow examples demonstrated in the book:

- Code::Blocks version 12.11.
- wxWidgets version 2.9.5
- conio2 library

A compiled copy of the wxWidgets library and conio2 library is provided with this book for your convenience.

Who this book is for

The target audience of this book is C/C++ developers. Prior knowledge of C/C++ compiler is required. This book is suitable for developers who want to learn about Code::Blocks and app development in C++ using it.

Conventions

In this book, you will find a number of styles of text that distinguish between different kinds of information. Here are some examples of these styles, and an explanation of their meaning.

Code words in text are shown as follows: "We can include other contexts through the use of the include directive."

A block of code is set as follows:

```
#include <iostream>

int main() {
  std::cout << "Hello World!" << std::endl;
  return 0;
}
```

Any command-line input or output is written as follows:

```
g++ -o app4.exe -g -O2 main.cpp
```

New **terms** and **important words** are shown in bold. Words that you see on the screen, in menus or dialog boxes for example, appear in the text like this: "clicking the **Next** button moves you to the next screen".

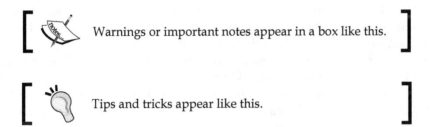

Warnings or important notes appear in a box like this.

Tips and tricks appear like this.

Reader feedback

Feedback from our readers is always welcome. Let us know what you think about this book—what you liked or may have disliked. Reader feedback is important for us to develop titles that you really get the most out of.

To send us general feedback, simply send an e-mail to feedback@packtpub.com, and mention the book title via the subject of your message.

If there is a topic that you have expertise in and you are interested in either writing or contributing to a book, see our author guide on www.packtpub.com/authors.

Customer support

Now that you are the proud owner of a Packt book, we have a number of things to help you to get the most from your purchase.

Downloading the example code

You can download the example code files for all Packt books you have purchased from your account at http://www.packtpub.com. If you purchased this book elsewhere, you can visit http://www.packtpub.com/support and register to have the files e-mailed directly to you.

Errata

Although we have taken every care to ensure the accuracy of our content, mistakes do happen. If you find a mistake in one of our books—maybe a mistake in the text or the code—we would be grateful if you would report this to us. By doing so, you can save other readers from frustration and help us improve subsequent versions of this book. If you find any errata, please report them by visiting http://www.packtpub.com/submit-errata, selecting your book, clicking on the **errata submission form** link, and entering the details of your errata. Once your errata are verified, your submission will be accepted and the errata will be uploaded on our website, or added to any list of existing errata, under the Errata section of that title. Any existing errata can be viewed by selecting your title from http://www.packtpub.com/support.

Piracy

Piracy of copyright material on the Internet is an ongoing problem across all media. At Packt, we take the protection of our copyright and licenses very seriously. If you come across any illegal copies of our works, in any form, on the Internet, please provide us with the location address or website name immediately so that we can pursue a remedy.

Please contact us at copyright@packtpub.com with a link to the suspected pirated material.

We appreciate your help in protecting our authors, and our ability to bring you valuable content.

Questions

You can contact us at questions@packtpub.com if you are having a problem with any aspect of the book, and we will do our best to address it.

1
Getting Started with Code::Blocks

While writing this book, Code::Blocks—12.11 was the latest stable release available. This release comes with GCC 4.7.1 compiler for Windows. We'll use this release for C++ development throughout this book. In this chapter, we'll download Code::Blocks, install and learn more about it.

Why Code::Blocks?

Before we go on learning more about **Code::Blocks** let us understand why we shall use Code::Blocks over other IDEs.

- It is a cross-platform Integrated Development Environment (IDE). It supports Windows, Linux, and Mac operating system.

- It supports GCC compiler and GNU debugger on all supported platforms completely.

- It supports numerous other compilers to various degrees on multiple platforms.

- It is scriptable and extendable. It comes with several plugins that extend its core functionality.

- It is lightweight on resources and doesn't require a powerful computer to run it.

- Finally, it is free and open source.

Installing Code::Blocks on Windows

Our primary focus of this book will be on Windows platform. However, we'll touch upon other platforms wherever possible. Official Code::Blocks binaries are available from www.codeblocks.org. Perform the following steps for successful installation of Code::Blocks:

1. For installation on Windows platform download codeblocks-12.11mingw-setup.exe file from http://www.codeblocks.org/downloads/26 or from sourceforge mirror http://sourceforge.net/projects/codeblocks/files/Binaries/12.11/Windows/codeblocks-12.11mingw-setup.exe/download and save it in a folder.

2. Double-click on this file and run it. You'll be presented with the following screen:

3. As shown in the following screenshot click on the **Next** button to continue. License text will be presented. The Code::Blocks application is licensed under GNU GPLv3 and Code::Blocks SDK is licensed under GNU LGPLv3. You can learn more about these licenses at this URL — https://www.gnu.org/licenses/licenses.html.

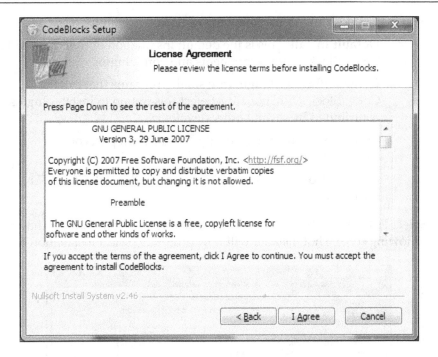

4. Click on **I Agree** to accept the License Agreement. The component selection page will be presented in the following screenshot:

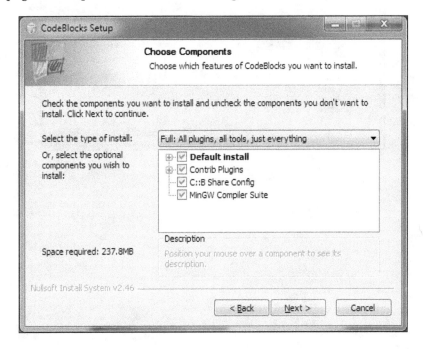

5. You may choose any of the following options:

   ° **Default install**: This is the default installation option. This will install Code::Block's core components and core plugins.

   ° **Contrib Plugins**: Plugins are small programs that extend Code::Block's functionality. Select this option to install plugins contributed by several other developers.

   ° **C::B Share Config**: This utility can copy all/parts of configuration file.

   ° **MinGW Compiler Suite**: This option will install GCC 4.7.1 for Windows.

6. Select **Full Installation** and click on **Next** button to continue. As shown in the following screenshot installer will now prompt to select installation directory:

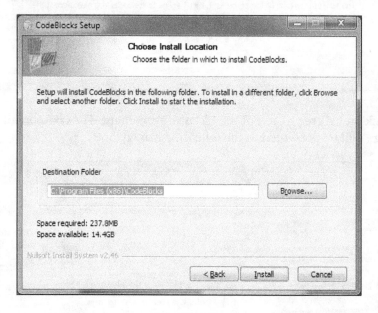

7. You can install it to default installation directory. Otherwise choose **Destination Folder** and then click on the **Install** button. Installer will now proceed with installation.

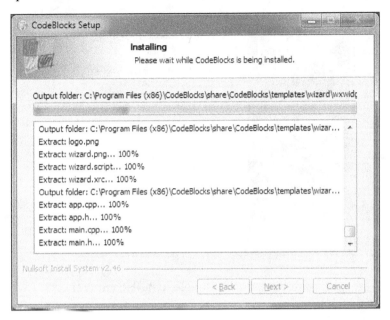

8. As shown in the following screenshot Code::Blocks will now prompt us to run it after the installation is completed:

9. Click on the **No** button here and then click on the **Next** button. Installation will now be completed:

10. Click on the **Finish** button to complete installation. A shortcut will be created on the desktop.

This completes our Code::Blocks installation on Windows.

Installing Code::Blocks on Linux

Code::Blocks runs numerous Linux distributions. In this section we'll learn about installation of Code::Blocks on CentOS linux. CentOS is a Linux distro based on Red Hat Enterprise Linux and is a freely available, enterprise grade Linux distribution. Perform the following steps to install Code::Blocks on Linux OS:

1. Navigate to **Settings | Administration | Add/Remove Software** menu option. Enter wxGTK in the Search box and hit the *Enter* key. As of writing wxGTK-2.8.12 is the latest wxWidgets stable release available. Select it and click on the **Apply** button to install wxGTK package via the package manager, as shown in the following screenshot.

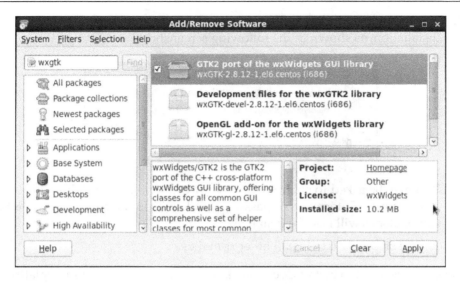

2. Download packages for **CentOS 6** from this URL—http://www.
    codeblocks.org/downloads/26.

    Unpack the .tar.bz2 file by issuing the following command in shell:

    ```
    tar xvjf codeblocks-12.11-1.el6.i686.tar.bz2
    ```

3. Right-click on the codeblocks-12.11-1.el6.i686.rpm file as shown in the
    following screenshot and choose the **Open with Package Installer** option.

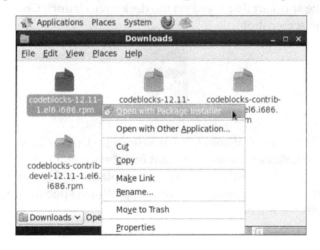

4. The following window will be displayed. Click on the **Install** button to begin installation, as shown in the following screenshot:

5. You may be asked to enter the root password if you are installing it from a user account. Enter the root password and click on the **Authenticate** button. Code::Blocks will now be installed.

6. Repeat steps 4 to 6 to install other rpm files.

We have now learned to install Code::Blocks on the Windows and Linux platforms. We are now ready for C++ development. Before doing that we'll learn about the Code::Blocks user interface.

First run

On the Windows platform navigate to the **Start** | **All Programs** | **CodeBlocks** | **CodeBlocks** menu options to launch Code::Blocks. Alternatively you may double-click on the shortcut displayed on the desktop to launch Code::Blocks, as in the following screenshot:

On Linux navigate to **Applications** | **Programming** | **Code::Blocks IDE** menu options to run Code::Blocks. Please note that in subsequent chapters of this book we'll limit our discussion mostly to the Windows platform. However, usage of Code::Blocks and C++ development (excluding platform specific areas) remain the same over both platforms.

Code::Blocks will now ask the user to select the default compiler. Code::Blocks supports several compilers and hence, is able to detect the presence of other compilers. The following screenshot shows that Code::Blocks has detected GNU GCC Compiler (which was bundled with the installer and has been installed). Click on it to select and then click on **Set as default button**, as shown in the following screenshot:

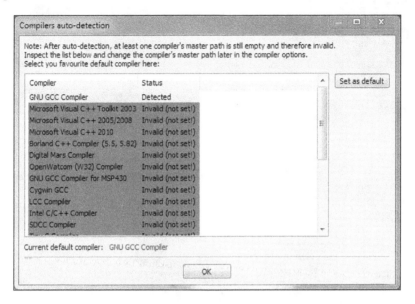

Do not worry about the items highlighted in red in the previous screenshot. Red colored lines indicate Code::Blocks was unable to detect the presence of a particular compiler.

Finally, click on the **OK** button to continue with the loading of Code::Blocks. After the loading is complete the Code::Blocks window will be shown.

The following screenshot shows main window of Code::Blocks. Annotated portions highlight different User Interface (UI) components:

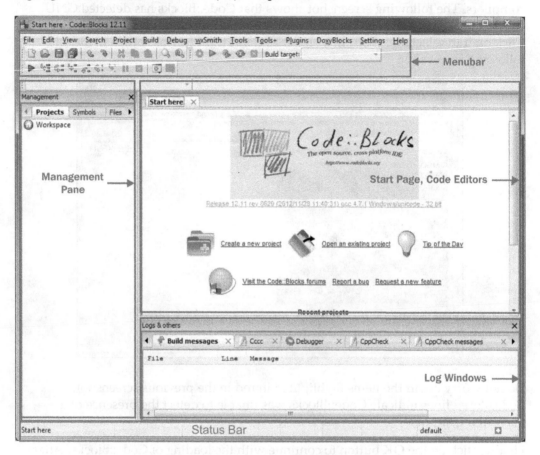

Now, let us understand more about different UI components:

- **Menu bar and toolbar**: All Code::Blocks commands are available via menu bar. On the other hand toolbars provide quick access to commonly used commands.

- **Start page and code editors**: Start page is the default page when Code::Blocks is launched. This contains some useful links and recent project and file history. Code editors are text containers to edit C++ (and other language) source files. These editors offer syntax highlighting—a feature that highlights keywords in different colors.

- **Management pane**: This window shows all open files (including source files, project files, and workspace files). This pane is also used by other plugins to provide additional functionalities. In the preceding screenshot **FileManager** plugin is providing a Windows Explorer like facility and **Code Completion** plugin is providing details of currently open source files.

- **Log windows**: Log messages from different tools, for example, compiler, debugger, document parser, and so on, are shown here. This component is also used by other plugins.

- **Status bar**: This component shows various status information of Code::Blocks, for example, file path, file encoding, line numbers, and so on.

Introduction to important toolbars

Toolbars provide easier access to different functions of Code::Blocks. Amongst the several toolbars following ones are most important.

Main toolbar

The main toolbar holds core component commands. From left to right there are new file, open file, save, save all, undo, redo, cut, copy, paste, find, and replace buttons.

Compiler toolbar

The compiler toolbar holds commonly used compiler related commands. From left to right there are build, run, build and run, rebuild, stop build, build target buttons. Compilation of C++ source code is also called a build and this terminology will be used throughout the book.

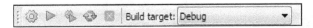

Debugger toolbar

The debugger toolbar holds commonly used debugger related commands. From left to right there are debug/continue, run to cursor, next line, step into, step out, next instruction, step into instruction, break debugger, stop debugger, debugging windows, and various info buttons.

Summary

In this chapter we learnt to download and install Code::Blocks. We also learnt about different interface elements. In the next chapter we shall start coding in C++ with Code::Blocks.

2
App Development with Code::Blocks

In this chapter, we'll learn C++ app development with Code::Blocks. We'll begin with a simple Hello World app. Subsequently concept of project and workspace will be introduced.

Creating your first app with Code::Blocks

Let's write a simple Hello World app, which essentially prints out "Hello World" to console. Launch Code::Blocks to begin and as shown in the following screenshot click on the new button in main toolbar and then click on the **File** menu option. The following screenshot represents the same:

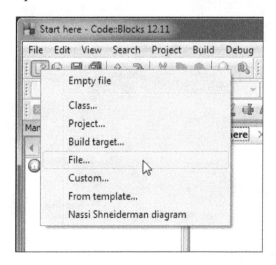

Click on the **C/C++ source** option in the next window and then on the **Go** button. A wizard will be presented. Click on the **Next** button on the first page of the wizard. Choose the **C++** option and click on the **Next** button. Choose file path and name in the next window and click on the **Finish** button to complete wizard.

Then type the following code in the editor:

```
#include <iostream>

int main() {
  std::cout << "Hello World!" << std::endl;
  return 0;
}
```

Code::Blocks will automatically add an empty line at the end of the file if there isn't any, this is a Code::Blocks feature. GCC expects an empty line at the end of source code, and it will throw warning if an empty line is missing. Thus you may notice an empty line is being added automatically by Code::Blocks.

After the code is typed in the editor window Code::Blocks will look similar to the following screenshot.

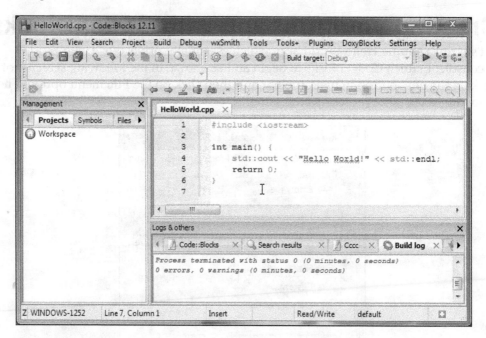

Now click on the save button in main toolbar to save this file (navigate to **File | Save** from the dropdown menu bar). Alternatively *Ctrl + S* key combination can be used to save a file. We can see that Code::Blocks has applied syntax highlighting to the code and it has made the code more readable.

Now click on the build button in the Compiler toolbar or hit *Ctrl + F9* key combination to compile it. If everything goes well Code::Blocks will look similar to the previous screenshot. Now click on the run button in Compiler toolbar. Code::Blocks will now run the program. As seen in the following screenshot our first program has run successfully:

The previous screenshot shows that the program execution has been completed and it is waiting for user input to close the window. This is a Code::Blocks feature which stops after the execution is completed in order to allow the users to study program output.

Our first assignment is successful. However, this approach has several drawbacks.

- Code::Blocks applies global compiler/linker flags during compilation of individual files
- Code::Blocks behaves purely as a text editor (imagine Notepad) and most features can't be used to compile individual files.

Also management of large projects comprising of individual files is cumbersome. So the concept of **Project** has evolved. In the next section we'll learn more about projects in Code::Blocks.

Project in Code::Blocks

The project is an important concept in Code::Blocks. A project can be described as a collection of source files and build targets.

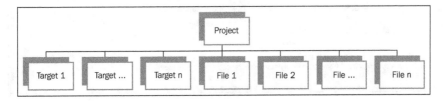

A build target can be defined as a label or a tag for each source file, which contains separate set of build (compiler, linker and resource compiler) options. Each build target contains a set of build options and during compilation of a project Code::Blocks selects currently active target. All files of that target is then compiled using that build target's build options.

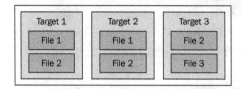

A project requires a minimum of one target and one source file to compile. A source file may be part of all or none of the targets. Build targets can be dependent upon other targets, which in turn helps to maintain a relationship between different source files. We'll explain a bit more on importance of build targets in the next section.

But before doing that let's create a project and develop an app. Perform the following steps for the same:

1. Click on the new button in the main toolbar, then click on the **Project** menu option. A wizard will be presented, as shown in the following screenshot. Now select **Console application** and click on the **Go** button:

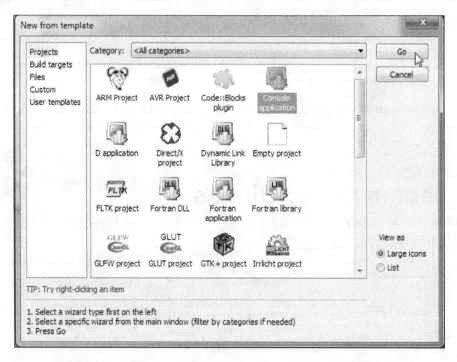

2. Click on the **Next** button on the first page of the wizard. Then choose **C++** and click on the **Next** button as shown in the following screenshot:

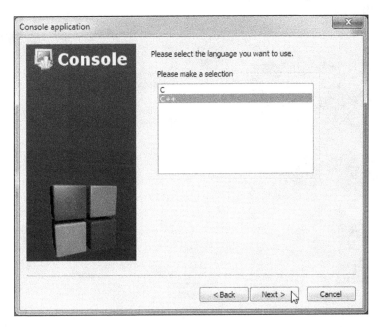

3. As shown in the following screenshot enter **Project title** (app name) as App1 and choose a folder to create App1 project. Now, click on the **Next** button to continue.

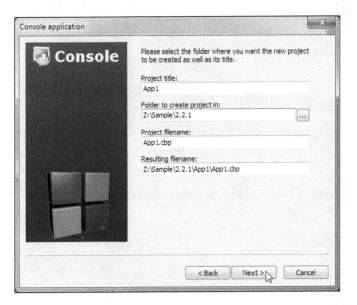

4. Click on the **Finish** button in the **Console application** window as shown in the following screenshot and the project will be generated with a default code:

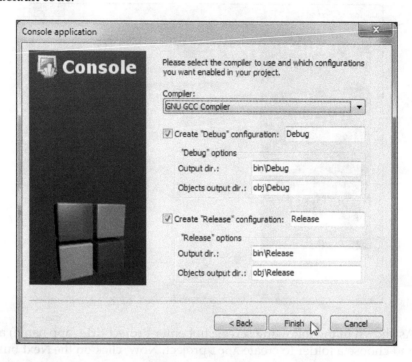

The following screenshot shows the **Management** window that has been populated with the newly created project files. Double-click on the main.cpp item on the tree to open the Code::Blocks editor.

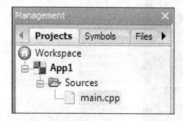

Let's replace the default code with the following code:

```
#include <iostream>

class HelloWorld {
public:
  HelloWorld() {}
```

```cpp
    ~HelloWorld() {}

    void Print() {
      std::cout << "Hello World!" << std::endl;
    }
};

int main()
{
    HelloWorld hello;
    hello.Print();
    return 0;
}
```

We have replaced earlier `HelloWorld` code with a code using **Object Oriented Programming (OOP)** concepts of C++. We have used C++ classes to achieve the same goal of printing "Hello World!" text.

C++ classes are specific data types that can be defined as a collection of data structure and member functions that operate on these data structures. All member functions and base classes are `private` by default. Classes can contain overloaded operator which allows customized operations associated with a particular class.

Classes can also be defined with a `struct` keyword. However, all members, that is, functions and base classes are `public` by default if a class is defined with a `struct` keyword.

Let's analyze our code. We have defined a class named `HelloWorld`. We have also defined a `constructor` function `HelloWorld()` and a `destructor` function `~HelloWorld()`. We have a publicly accessible function named `Print()` to print out "Hello World!" text. In the `main()` function we created an object named `hello` of class `HelloWorld` and then we have used it to call `Print()` function.

Hit *F9* key to build and then run this project. A console window will pop up displaying "Hello World!" text.

Project with multiple files

In this section we'll learn about C++ app development comprising of multiple files. We'll develop a class, called `Vector`, which implements a dynamic array. This class is similar to the `std::vector` class offered by **Standard Template Library (STL)** and has a very limited set of features compared to STL class.

Create a new project and name it App2. Navigate to **File | New | File...** menu option and then choose **C/C++ header** option and follow the wizard to add a new file to App2 project. Add the following code in a new file under App2 and name it vector.h file:

```
#ifndef __VECTOR_H__
#define __VECTOR_H__

#ifndef DATA_TYPE
#define DATA_TYPE double
#endif

class Vector {
public:
    Vector(size_t size = 2);
    virtual ~Vector();

    size_t GetCount() const;

    bool Set(size_t id, DATA_TYPE data);
    DATA_TYPE operator[] (size_t id);

private:
    DATA_TYPE* m_data;
    size_t     m_size;
};

#endif //__VECTOR_H__
```

Header file vector.h declares the Vector class structure. We have a pre-processor macro DATA_TYPE that defines the data type that this class holds. We have a constructor (with a default parameter) and a destructor function. These functions will allocate and de-allocate a pointer m_data that holds array of elements. A member variable m_size will be used to hold size of array that will assist us in bound-checking.

There are several member functions that operate on the member variables. The GetCount() function returns number array size, Set() function assigns a value to an element in array. An operator [] has been overloaded to access array data.

The `Vector` class has been implemented in the `vector.cpp` file. Create and add this new file to `App2` project and then copy the following code to it:

```cpp
#include <cstring>
#include "vector.h"

Vector::Vector(size_t size)
    : m_size(size)
{
    m_data = new DATA_TYPE[m_size];
    ::memset(m_data, 0, m_size * sizeof(DATA_TYPE));
}

Vector::~Vector() {
    if (m_data) {
        delete [] m_data;
        m_data = 0;
    }
}

size_t Vector::GetCount() const {
    return m_size;
}

bool Vector::Set(size_t id, DATA_TYPE data) {
    if (id < m_size) {
        m_data[id] = data;
        return true;
    }
    return false;
}

DATA_TYPE Vector::operator[](size_t id) {
    if (id < m_size) {
        return *(m_data + id);
    }

    return 0;
}
```

The line m_size(size) defines an initializer list. where member variables are initialized as per the order they have been declared. We have used new operator to allocate an array of size given by user. The memset() function initializes that array with zeroes. In destructor internal array is checked for null pointer and then de-allocated with delete [] keyword and assigned a null pointer.

> Null pointers have a value (typically 0) that is reserved to indicate that it doesn't point to any valid object. Any operation on null pointers will lead to a segmentation fault or access violation. In such a case, app will die instantly. C++ 11 defines a separate nullptr constant to define a null pointer.

There are two member functions, Set() and GetCount() that operate on the internal array.

Finally, replace code inside the main.cpp file with the following code. It creates an object of Vector class and subsequently uses it:

```cpp
#include <iostream>
#include "vector.h"

int main() {
    Vector vec(4);
    vec.Set(0, 10); // Set first item = 10
    vec.Set(2, 55); // Set first item = 55
    std::cout << "Number of elements = " << vec.GetCount() <<
std::endl;
    std::cout << "vec[1] = " << vec[1] << std::endl;
    std::cout << "vec[2] = " << vec[2] << std::endl;
    return 0;
}
```

Now, the **Management** window will look similar to the following screenshot:

We'll define a pre-processor define to ensure that the **Vector** class is compiled as an array of integers. Navigate to **Project | Build options...** menu option and the **Project build options** window will be presented:

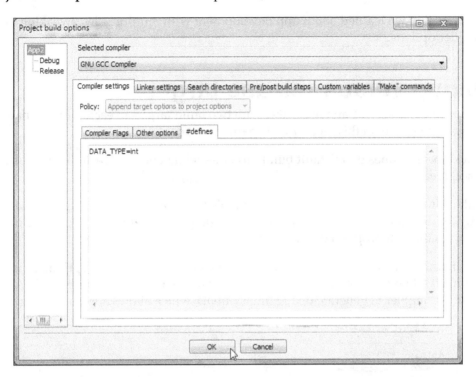

As we intend to apply the settings throughout the project click on the root of the project tree in that window. Now, click on the **Compiler settings | #defines** tab and add the line as per the preceding screenshot. Further, click on the **OK** button to close that dialog box. Now compile and run this project. This will produce result as per the following screenshot:

In our code we have a pre-processor macro DATA_TYPE that defines the data type that this class holds. If we intend to use it as an array of double we have to recompile this app.

Do note that pre-processor macros work by simple text substitution and no type checking is performed on them during substitution. This can introduce other bugs in the program if it is used incorrectly.

In this section we learned about app development with multiple files, tweaking of compiler options.

Debug versus release target

We noticed that in App1 and App2, there are two build targets in each project—namely **debug** and **release**. In this section we'll learn more about it.

Code::Blocks defines two default build targets—debug and release at the time of a project creation.

As the name suggests a debug target is suitable for app debugging. Appropriate compiler options are added to generate debugging symbols in the compiled app. It also disables all program optimizations.

We can find in the following screenshot (navigate to **Project | Build options...** menu option) a **Debug** target has a compiler option **Produce debugging symbols**. This instructs compiler to generate debugging symbols, which allows app debugging:

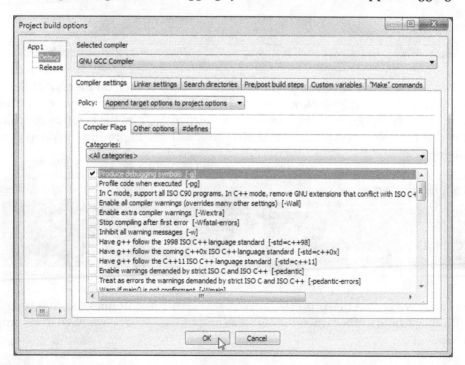

A **Release** target disables generation of debugging symbols. It also defines appropriate compiler options to optimize the program. Thus this is suitable for code to be used in production. The following screenshot shows typical compiler flags in a release target.

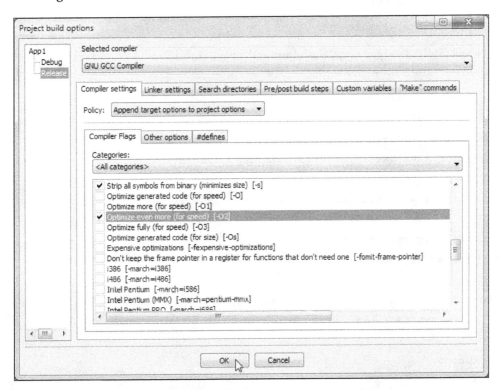

These two targets are quite important as it is difficult to debug a program that has been compiled with compiler optimization flags enabled. It is highly recommended that the program is compiled without optimization in debug target.

To understand this problem we'll use the following code snippet, then compile and debug it. Note that we will use command-line tools to avoid abstraction of any error message by Code::Blocks UI:

```cpp
#include <iostream>

int add (int a, int b) {
    return (a + b);
}

int main() {
```

```
    std::cout << "2 + 3 = " << add(2, 3) << std::endl;
    return 0;
}
```

Let's now compile it in debug mode:

```
g++ -o app4.exe -g main.cpp
```

We'll use GNU debugger gdb to debug and understand the flow of execution. Launch gdb and follow the steps:

```
gdb --quiet app4.exe
Reading symbols from Z:\app4.exe...done.
(gdb) b main.cpp:4
Breakpoint 1 at 0x401945: file main.cpp, line 4.
(gdb) b main.cpp:9
Breakpoint 2 at 0x4019ae: file main.cpp, line 9.
(gdb) r
Starting program: Z:\app4.exe
[New Thread 6036.0x6ac]

Breakpoint 1, add (a=2, b=3) at main.cpp:4
4        return (a + b);
(gdb) c
Continuing.
2 + 3 = 5

Breakpoint 2, _fu0___ZSt4cout () at main.cpp:9
9        return 0;
(gdb) c
Continuing.
[Inferior 1 (process 6036) exited normally]
```

We asked gdb to load app4.exe in memory. Then we asked gdb to set two **breakpoints** by issuing command b and specifying the line number. We asked gdb to run the program. As instructed by breakpoints the execution is paused at each breakpoint. Subsequently the program completes without any error.

Let's see what happens when we turn optimizations on. We'll compile it as:

```
g++ -o app4.exe -g -O2 main.cpp
```

Now debug this app again following earlier steps:

```
gdb --quiet app4.exe
Reading symbols from Z:\app4.exe...done.
(gdb) b main.cpp:4
Breakpoint 1 at 0x401574: file main.cpp, line 4.
(gdb) b main.cpp:9
Breakpoint 2 at 0x402883: main.cpp:9. (2 locations)
(gdb) r
Starting program: Z:\app4.exe
[New Thread 6084.0x1270]

Breakpoint 2, _GLOBAL__sub_I__Z3addii () at main.cpp:10
10    }
(gdb) c
Continuing.
2 + 3 = 5

Breakpoint 2, _fu0___ZSt4cout () at main.cpp:10
10    }
(gdb) c
Continuing.
[Inferior 1 (process 6084) exited normally]
```

It is evident from the preceding output that compiler has optimized our source code and made a number of changes to the code. The function add() seems to have been expanded inline. As a result breakpoint on line return (a + b) of main.cpp file is never hit during execution.

This is one of the side effects of optimization on debugging process. Code::Blocks creates two default targets to avoid similar situation. It is highly recommended that this is followed in project development.

Project with external library

In this section we'll develop an app with an external library. External libraries are used in almost every project written in any language. They allow code reuse resulting faster project cycle. We'll learn how to configure an external library with a Code::Blocks project.

We have printed `Hello World!` text to console. How about printing text in color? We can use a library called `conio2` (`http://conio.sourceforge.net/`) to print text in color and do other text manipulations. A compiled copy of `conio2` library is provided together with the book. Consider the following example code:

```
#include <cstring>
#include "conio2.h"

int main() {
    int screenWidth = 0;
    const char* msg = "Hello World!\n\n";
    struct text_info textInfo;
    inittextinfo();
    gettextinfo(&textInfo);
    screenWidth  = textInfo.screenwidth;
    textcolor(YELLOW);
    textbackground(RED);
    cputsxy( (screenWidth - strlen(msg))/2 , textInfo.cury, const_
cast<char*>(msg) );
    textcolor(WHITE); // Restore original colours
    textbackground(BLACK);
    return 0;
}
```

In this example we have included `conio2.h` file in second line. This will expose pre-defined functions in `conio2` library to our app. We have defined couple of variables namely `screenWidth`, `msg`, and `textInfo` inside `main()` function. We have then retrieved current console text settings using `gettextinfo()` function.

In the next line we have saved current screen width to `screenWidth` variable. Subsequently we have assigned `YELLOW` foreground color and `RED` background color. We have used the `cputsxy()` function to print desired text. We have then restored text colors in the subsequent two lines.

In order to set up external library navigate to **Projects | Build options...** menu option and click on the **Search directories** tab as shown in the following screenshot:

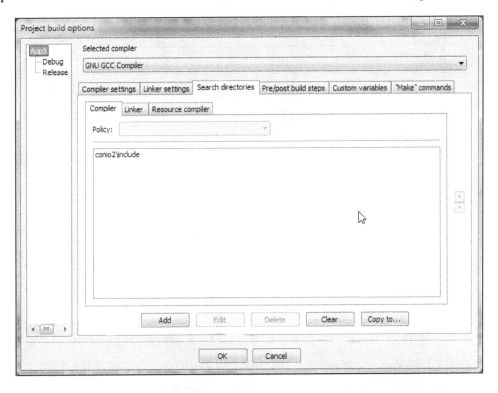

Add `conio2\include` path (relative to project path) as shown in the preceding screenshot. We can also use full path if `conio2` library is installed in another location. This will instruct compiler to also search this directory for any header files referred in the code.

Next click on the **Linker** tab as shown in the following screenshot and add the `conio2\lib` relative path as per the following screenshot. This will instruct linker to also search static library in this path.

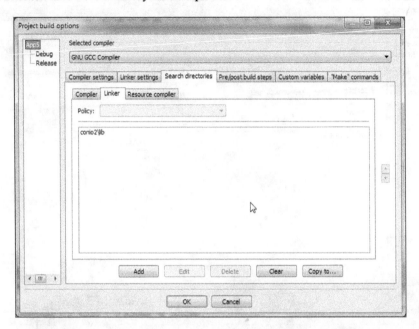

Click on the **Linker settings** tab and add `libconio.a` as per the following screenshot:

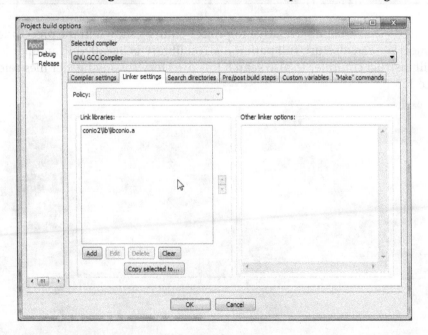

After this step is completed our app is ready for compilation. Now compile and run it. We'll see the following output:

Our app is now using an external C/C++ library. We can use other external libraries in a similar manner for our app development.

Workspace

Workspace in Code::Blocks is a collection of projects. Workspace acts as a container of projects and also maintains project dependencies. So if project 2 is dependent upon project 1, then project 2 will be compiled before compilation of project 1.

Consider the following snippets. Create a static library project named libcalc by navigating to **File | New | Project...** and select **Static library** wizard.

Then replace code of project's main.c file with the following code:

```
int mult(int a, int b)
{
    return (a * b);
}
```

Next create a console project named App6 and then replace its main.cpp file with the following code:

```
#include <iostream>

extern "C" int mult(int a, int b);

int main() {
    std::cout << "2 * 3 = " << mult(2, 3);
    return 0;
}
```

The **Management** window now shows two projects in one workspace. Workspace has been renamed to App6 in the following screenshot:

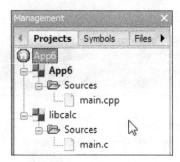

This workspace can be saved by navigating to **File** | **Save workspace as...** menu option. Right-click on the **App6** project in project tree and click on the Screenshot menu option. Next click on the **Project's dependencies** button. The following window will be presented:

Click on the **Close** button to close this window and then the **OK** button to close **Project/target options** window. Now App6 is dependent upon libcalc project.

Now navigate to **Project** | **Build options...** menu option and add ..\libcalc\ libcalc.a to **Link libraries** in **Linker settings** tab.

To compile these two projects navigate to the **Build** | **Build workspace** menu option. Code::Blocks will now build App6 taking care of its dependent project.

It is now quite clear that we can use workspace to manage sub-projects in a large project.

Summary

In this chapter we have learned to create project in Code::Blocks. We understood the importance of build targets. We also learned to use external libraries in our project. Finally, we learned to create and use a workspace.

With this we conclude our introduction to projects in Code::Blocks. We'll discuss debugging in the next chapter.

3
App Debugging with Code::Blocks

Debugging is an essential step in any app development. It is also an essential part of an IDE and Code::Blocks is no exception. It offers a vast set of features to make app debugging easier.

In this chapter, we will learn about app debugging with Code::Blocks. We'll begin with a simple app to show various features of Code::Blocks.

Introduction to debugging in Code::Blocks

Code::Blocks supports two debuggers:

- **GNU Debugger** or, as it is popularly known as **GDB**
- Microsoft **Console Debugger** or **CDB**

Code::Blocks installer bundles GDB together with GCC compiler. CDB can be downloaded and installed together with installation of Windows **Software Development Kit (SDK)** for Windows.

Windows SDK is a collection of tools offered by Microsoft for Microsoft Windows platform. It consists of compiler, headers, libraries, debugger, samples, documentation, and tools required to develop applications for .NET Framework.

CDB can be downloaded and installed from the following link:

`http://msdn.microsoft.com/en-us/library/windows/hardware/gg463009.aspx`

Our focus will be on GDB throughout this chapter. Debugger related functions are available via the **Debug** menu in Code::Blocks as shown in the following screenshot. A debugger toolbar is also provided for quicker access to commonly used functions.

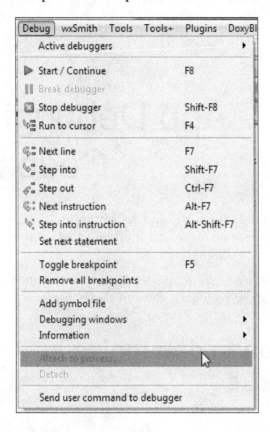

We can access several debugger related windows by navigating to **Debug | Debugging windows** menu options. The following screenshot shows available menu options.

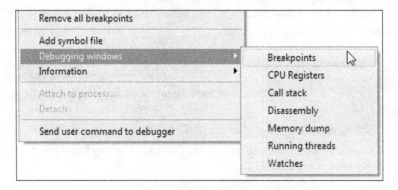

We can get more information about running process from **Debug | Information** and then clicking on appropriate menu option. The following screenshot shows available menu options:

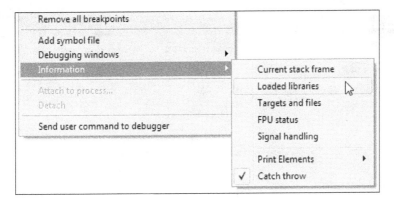

Debugger settings can be accessed by navigating to **Settings | Debugger** menu option. The following screenshot shows the debugger settings dialog:

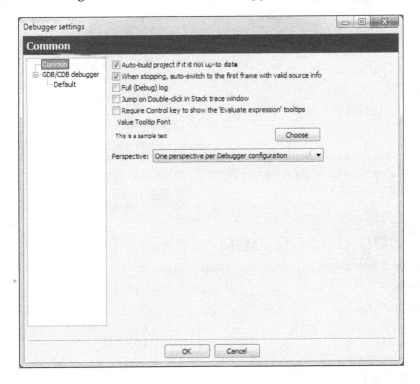

Select **Default** in the tree on the left-hand side and more debugger related options will be available as shown in the following screenshot:

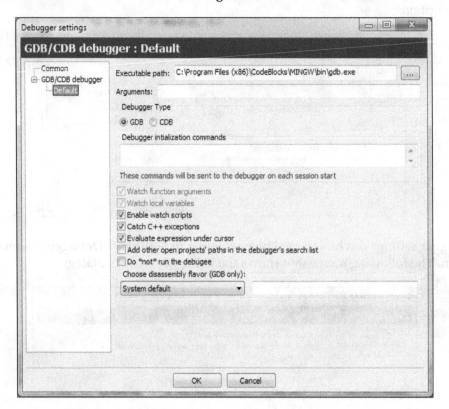

Select the **Evaluate expressions under cursor** option shown in the previous screenshot. This option will provide a tooltip containing details whenever cursor is moved over a variable.

First app debugging

Let us create a new console project App7 and replace code inside main.cpp file with following code:

```cpp
#include <iostream>

int main() {
    const double pi = 3.141592653589793238462643383832795;
    double radius  = 20.0;
    double perimeter= 0.0;
```

```
    perimeter = 2 * pi * radius;
    std::cout << "Perimeter = " << perimeter << std::endl;
    return 0;
}
```

Ensure that **Debug** target is selected in compiler toolbar and then compile it by clicking compile button. `App7` will be compiled for debugging.

Before we ask GDB to debug we have to create breakpoints for it. After the code is typed in editor window Code::Blocks will look similar to the following screenshot.

```
main.cpp  ×
 1      #include <iostream>
 2
 3     int main() {
 4          const double pi = 3.1415926535897932384626433832795;
 5          double radius    = 20.0;
 6          double perimeter= 0.0;
 7          perimeter = 2 * pi * radius;
 8          std::cout << "Perimeter = " << perimeter << std::endl;
 9          return 0;
10     }
11
```

To set a breakpoint move cursor to the left side of editor window next to the indicated line numbers. Now the cursor will change to a right-tilted cursor. Pause mouse and left-click. A breakpoint will be set there and will be indicated by a red circle. The following screenshot shows that a breakpoint has been set at line number 4.

```
main.cpp  ×
 1      #include <iostream>
 2
 3     int main() {
 4          const double pi = 3.1415926535897932384626433832795;
 5          double radius    = 20.0;
 6          double perimeter= 0.0;
 7          perimeter = 2 * pi * radius;
 8          std::cout << "Perimeter = " << perimeter << std::endl;
 9          return 0;
10     }
11
```

Next follow same method and create breakpoints at line numbers 5, 6 and 9. Editor window will now look similar to the following screenshot:

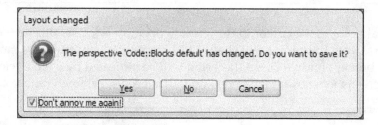

```
main.cpp  X
1          #include <iostream>
2
3        ⊟int main() {
4 ●          const double pi = 3.1415926535897932384626433832795;
5 ●          double radius    = 20.0;
6 ●          double perimeter= 0.0;
7           perimeter = 2 * pi * radius;
8           std::cout << "Perimeter = " << perimeter << std::endl;
9 ●          return 0;
10         }
```

All breakpoints are now visually indicated in the editor window.

We can now start debugging by clicking on the **Debug/Continue** button in debugger toolbar. Alternatively the *F8* key may be used to start debugging. The following window may appear:

Layout changed

The perspective 'Code::Blocks default' has changed. Do you want to save it?

Yes   No   Cancel

☑ Don't annoy me again!

This highlights that default layout of Code::Blocks has changed as the **Debugger log** window has received focus (refer to the preceding screenshot). Select the **Don't annoy me again!** checkbox and then click on **No** button to stop it. It won't appear again. Let's look at the entire IDE now.

In the following screenshot execution has stopped at line number 4 and the cursor has changed to a yellow colored triangle. This indicates that debugger has stopped execution at that position. Debugger log window will also be updated when we continue debugging.

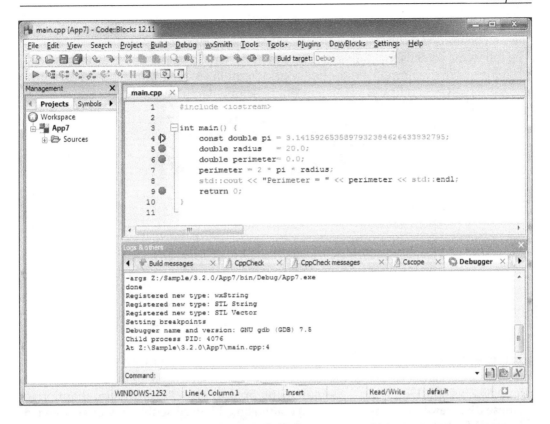

Before continuing with debugging we take a look at debugger related features of Code::Blocks. **CPU Registers** can be examined by navigating to the **Debug | Debugging windows | CPU Registers** menu option. A register is a tiny but a high speed buffer embedded within the processor hardware.

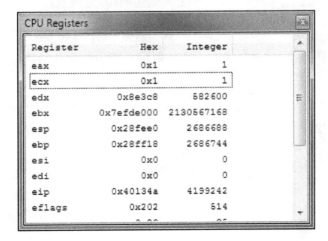

Now navigate to the **Debug | Debugging windows | Disassembly** menu option; this can be used to display assembly language representation of current C++ code. The following screenshot shows the **Disassembly** window and also indicates the position where execution has stopped. Clicking on the **Mixed Mode** checkbox will superimpose C++ code and corresponding assembly language code:

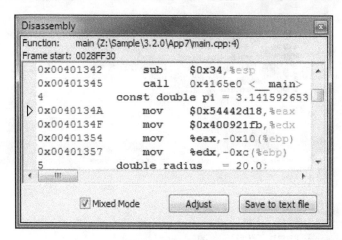

This style of assembly language is known as **AT&T** style. We can switch to **Intel** style assembly language in the disassembly dialog by navigating to the **Settings | Debugger | GDB/Debugger | Default** menu option and selecting the **Intel** option in **Choose disassembly flavor** (GDB only) combo box. Now close the previously opened disassembly dialog and reopen it. It will now show disassembly in Intel flavor as shown in the following screenshot. Please note that the choice of AT&T or Intel style is up to the preference of a developer. It has no effect on the debugging process.

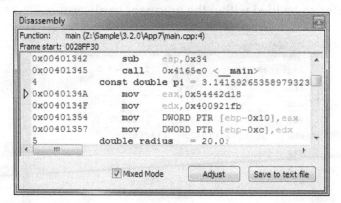

Currently running threads can be examined by navigating to **Debug | Debugging windows | Running threads** menu option. This app is single threaded and thus in the following screenshot we find that only one thread is running:

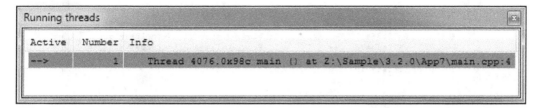

Stack frame can be examined by navigating to **Debug | Information | Current stack frame** menu option. Call stack is a data structure that stores information about current running function. The following screenshot shows the stack frame information of current process:

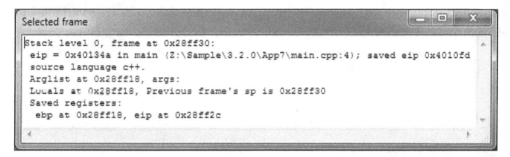

Call stack is a data structure that works on the principle of (**Last In First Out**) and stores information about active subroutines or program. Stack frame is part of call stack that stores information (local variables, return address and function parameters) of a single subroutine or function.

Whenever an app is run on Windows platform several **Dynamic Link Libraries (DLL)** or dynamic libraries are loaded in memory. DLL provide functions that are accessible by other apps without including a copy of function code inside the apps using it. Loaded libraries can be examined by navigating to **Debug | Information | Loaded libraries** menu option.

The following screenshot shows the loaded libraries for our app:

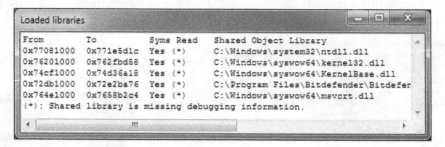

The asterisk next to the DLL name indicates whether their source can be debugged. We find that none of them allows debugging.

Now we'll continue with debugging after our introduction to several debugger related windows. We'll also learn to set watch on a variable. Click on the **Continue** button and debugger will stop at line number 5. Right-click on radius variable in editor window and then choose watch 'radius' menu option.

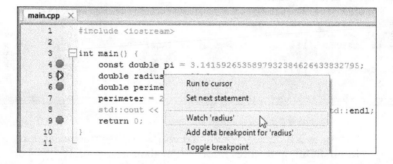

This will create a watch on the variable radius. A watch can be defined as an instruction to the debugger to track a variable during execution of an app. A separate window with the variable under watch will now be opened as shown in the following screenshot. Watch window can also be opened via **Debug | Debugging Windows | Watches** menu option:

If we click on the **Continue** button again then execution of app will advance to next line. This will update content of the radius variable in our app. Watch window will also update its content showing current value of the radius variable as shown in the following screenshot:

At this step we'll learn about another type of breakpoint known as **data breakpoint**. Right-click on the radius variable in line number 5 in editor window shown in the following screenshot and then click on the **Add data breakpoint for 'radius'** menu option:

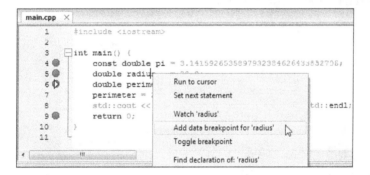

Select **Break on read or write** option as in the following screenshot and click on the **OK** button. By doing this we are instructing GDB to pause execution whenever the radius variable is read or written.

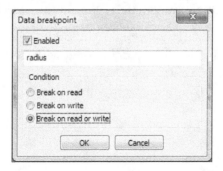

A data breakpoint will now be created. However data breakpoint is not shown visually in editor window. It can be verified from **Breakpoints** window by navigating to the **Debug | Debugging windows | Breakpoints** menu option. Last line in the following screenshot shows that a data breakpoint has been set.

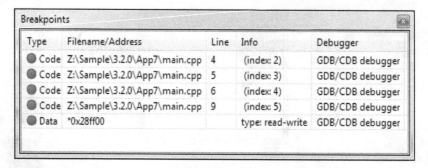

Click on the **Continue** button in debugger toolbar or press the *F8* key and execution will continue. It will now stop at line 7 due to the data breakpoint we have set in previous step. Variable radius is being read at this line and gdb has stopped execution as data breakpoint condition has been met.

```cpp
main.cpp  X
1      #include <iostream>
2
3      int main() {
4          const double pi = 3.1415926535897932384626433832795;
5          double radius    = 20.0;
6          double perimeter= 0.0;
7          perimeter = 2 * pi * radius;
8          std::cout << "Perimeter = " << perimeter << std::endl;
9          return 0;
10     }
```

Click on the **Continue** button to continue execution of app and subsequently it will stop at line number 9. If we continue clicking on the **Continue** button app, execution will stop several times due to the data breakpoint we have set earlier. This is normal and in order to stop execution immediately click on the **Stop** button in debugger toolbar or press *Shift + F8* key to stop execution.

This completes our introduction to app debugging with Code::Blocks.

Multiple app debugging

Real life projects are large in size and may consist of several sub-projects. It is essential that an IDE allows debugging of large apps spanning across several projects. With Code::Blocks we can do it easily.

To learn multiple app debugging we'll create two projects—first project a DLL project and second one is a console project that depends upon first DLL project. Then save both projects under same workspace named App8.

Go to **File | New | Project | Dynamic Link Library** menu option to create a DLL project. Name this project libobject. Now rename the libobject project files. We'll rename main.h file to dllmain.h and main.cpp to dllmain.cpp file. To do this, close all open editor files and right-click on the file name in the project tree as shown in the following screenshot:

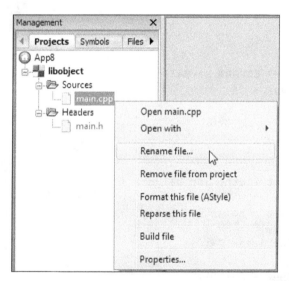

Enter new file name in the dialog box shown in following screenshot:

This will avoid ambiguities in file names. Now replace code inside `dllmain.h` file with the following code.

```
#ifndef __DLLMAIN_H__
#define __DLLMAIN_H__

/*  To use this exported function of dll, include this header
 *  in your project.
 */

#ifdef BUILD_DLL
    #define DLL_IMP_EXPORT __declspec(dllexport)
#else
    #define DLL_IMP_EXPORT __declspec(dllimport)
#endif

#ifdef __cplusplus
extern "C"
{
#endif
    void DLL_IMP_EXPORT SayHello(void);
#ifdef __cplusplus
}
#endif

class base {
public:
    void Set(int width, int height) {
        m_width  = width;
        m_height = height;
    }
    virtual int Area() = 0;
protected:
    int m_width, m_height;
};

class DLL_IMP_EXPORT Rectangle : public base {
public:
    int Area();
};

class DLL_IMP_EXPORT Triangle : public base {
public:
    int Area();
};

#endif // __DLLMAIN_H__
```

A DLL on Windows require special decoration in order to export it from a dynamic link library. This decoration statement changes while it is exported and at the time it is imported. Decoration `__declspec(dllexport)` is used to export functions from a DLL and `__declspec(dllimport)` is used to import function from another DLL. Decorations instruct linker to export or import a variable/function/object name with or without name mangling. A preprocessor define `DLL_IMP_EXPORT` is used to indicate compiler whether a function or a class is being exported or imported.

C++ allows function/method overloading. It is achieved by introducing name mangling in the generated code. Name mangling is a process in which a function name is converted to a unique name based on function parameters, return type, and other parameters. Name mangling is compiler dependent and as a result any DLL written is C++ can't be used directly with another compiler.

C++ introduces name mangling by default for all functions. We can stop name mangling using `extern "C"` keyword and are using it to stop name mangling for the exported `SayHello()` function. By stopping name mangling we can use a DLL written in C++ and compiled with one compiler to be used with another compiler.

We have defined a class `base` and this `base` class has a member function `Set()` and it sets two internal variables. There is a pure virtual function named `Area()` that must be redefined derived classes. A **pure virtual function** is a function that has not been implemented in the base class. If a pure virtual function is called in any app it may result in a crash.

However, this `base` class is not decorated with `DLL_IMP_EXPORT`. This means it will not be exported in DLL and no outside app can use this class.

In order to use feature of the `base` class we'll create two derived classes. Class `Rectangle` and `Triangle`, these are derived publicly from the `base` class. We have used inheritance of classes here. These classes are declared with decoration `DLL_IMP_EXPORT`. Thus these two classes will be exported in the resulting DLL.

Now replace code inside the `dllmain.cpp` file of the `libobject` project with the following code:

```
#include <windows.h>
#include <iostream>

#include "dllmain.h"

void SayHello(void) {
    std::cout << "Hello World!" << std::endl;
}
```

```
int Rectangle::Area() {
    return (m_width * m_height);
}

int Triangle::Area() {
    return (m_width * m_height / 2);
}

extern "C" DLL_IMP_EXPORT BOOL APIENTRY DllMain(HINSTANCE hinstDLL,
DWORD fdwReason, LPVOID lpvReserved) {
    switch (fdwReason) {
        case DLL_PROCESS_ATTACH: // attach to process
            // return FALSE to fail DLL load
            break;
        case DLL_PROCESS_DETACH: // detach from process
            break;
        case DLL_THREAD_ATTACH: // attach to thread
            break;
        case DLL_THREAD_DETACH: // detach from thread
            break;
    }
    return TRUE; // successful
}
```

Code in the dllmain.cpp file mainly defines all the code of publicly exported function. There is a DllMain() function. It may be used to do any initialization or de-initialization for the DLL.

Next create a console app named App8. Now rename workspace as App8 and save workspace as App8. This console app will use functions defined in libobject.dll. Replace code inside the main.cpp file of App8 with the following code:

```
#include <iostream>

#include "dllmain.h"

int main() {
    Rectangle rect;
    rect.Set(10, 20);
    Triangle trigl;
    trigl.Set(5, 6);
    std::cout << "Rectangle(10, 20).Area() = " << rect.Area() <<
std::endl;
    std::cout << "Triangle(5, 6).Area() = " << trigl.Area() <<
std::endl;
    return 0;
}
```

Next, we have to prepare our `App8` project to use this DLL. To do so go to **Project |
Build options** menu option. Select `App8` in the project tree and then click on **Search
directories** tab. Then add `..\libobject` directory to the list in the **Compiler** tab.
This instructs compiler to search for header files in that directory:

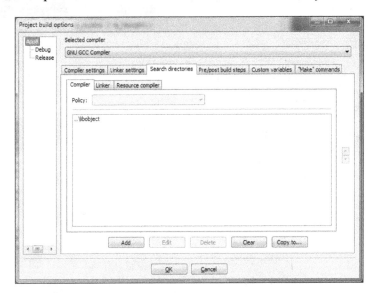

We also need to point linker to the directory where we have kept import library
of `libobject.dll` file. To do so select the **Debug** target and click on the **Search
directories** tab. Then click on the **Linker** tab and add `..\libobject\bin\Debug`
folder to the list:

We have to instruct linker to find references of symbols found in `libobject.dll` file. To do so click on the **Linker settings** tab and add `libobject.a` to the **Link libraries** list.

We'll set up project dependencies in this step. Go to **Project | Properties...** menu option and then click on the **Project dependencies...** button. Click on the `libobject` and then click on the **Close** button. Finally click **OK** button to close the **Project/ targets** options window. This completes preparation of the App8 console app.

Now go to **Build | Build workspace** menu option. This will build the `libobject` project first and subsequently App8 will be compiled.

In order to learn debugging multiple projects we'll set breakpoints at the following line number:

- Line number 11, 15, 19 in the `dllmain.cpp` file, `libobject` project
- Line number 7, 9, 10, 12 in the `main.cpp` file, `App8` project

Breakpoints can be verified from **Breakpoints** window shown in the following screenshot:

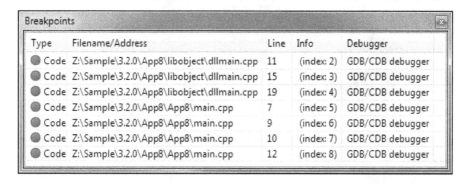

Note that DLLs can't run as a standalone process and require a host application to load them into memory. In order to debug a DLL we have to debug the host application that loads and runs it. Alternatively we can specify a host application (in our case `App8.exe`) for debugging by navigating to **Project | Set programs' arguments...** menu option.

We'll use first approach and let our host app to load `libobject.dll`, then use it to debug both `libobject.dll` and `App8.exe` file. Ensure that `App8` project is activated in the project tree and then click on the debug/continue button in debugger toolbar:

```
dllmain.h    ×  dllmain.cpp   ×  main.cpp    ×
 9
10      int Rectangle::Area() {
11  ●       return (m_width * m_height);
12      }
13
14      int Triangle::Area() {
15  ●       return (m_width * m_height / 2);
16      }
17
18      extern "C" DLL_IMP_EXPORT BOOL APIENTRY DllMain(
19  ◗      switch (fdwReason) {
20             case DLL_PROCESS_ATTACH: // attach to pr
```

In the preceding screenshot execution has stopped at line number `19` of the `dllmain.cpp` file. Whenever `DllMain()` is exported it becomes the first function to be called during the loading/unloading of any DLL. As a result execution stops there.

Loaded libraries window in the following screenshot confirms that `libobject.dll` has been loaded in memory and this library can be debugged:

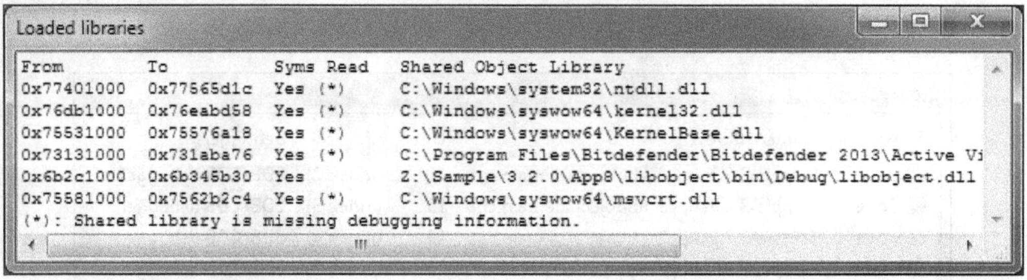

Loaded libraries
From To Syms Read Shared Object Library
0x77401000 0x77565d1c Yes (*) C:\Windows\system32\ntdll.dll
0x76db1000 0x76eabd58 Yes (*) C:\Windows\syswow64\kernel32.dll
0x75531000 0x75576a18 Yes (*) C:\Windows\syswow64\KernelBase.dll
0x73131000 0x731aba76 Yes (*) C:\Program Files\Bitdefender\Bitdefender 2013\Active Vi
0x6b2c1000 0x6b345b30 Yes Z:\Sample\3.2.0\App8\libobject\bin\Debug\libobject.dll
0x75581000 0x7562b2c4 Yes (*) C:\Windows\syswow64\msvcrt.dll
(*): Shared library is missing debugging information.

Click on the **Continue** button to continue. Execution will now pause at line number `7` of the `main.cpp` file.

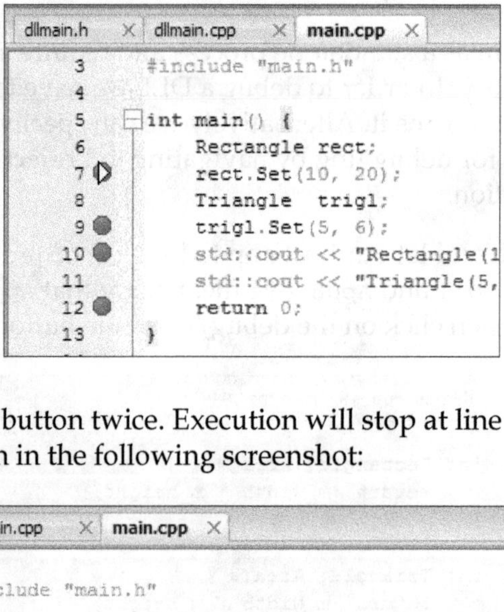

dllmain.h
dllmain.cpp
main.cpp
3 #include "main.h"
4
5 int main() {
6 Rectangle rect;
7 rect.Set(10, 20);
8 Triangle trigl;
9 trigl.Set(5, 6);
10 std::cout << "Rectangle(1
11 std::cout << "Triangle(5,
12 return 0;
13 }

Click on the **Continue** button twice. Execution will stop at line number `10` of the `main.cpp` file as shown in the following screenshot:

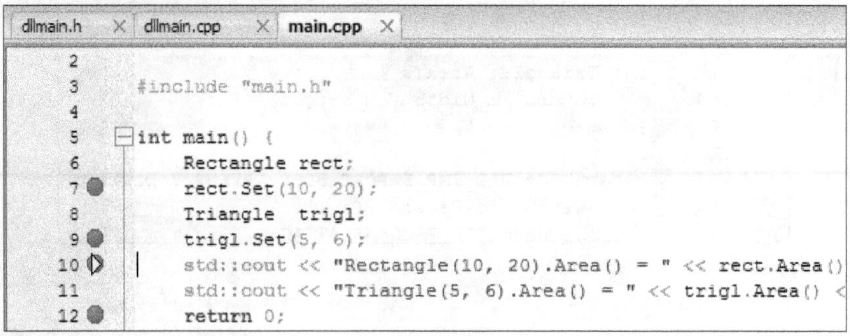

dllmain.h
dllmain.cpp
main.cpp
2
3 #include "main.h"
4
5 int main() {
6 Rectangle rect;
7 rect.Set(10, 20);
8 Triangle trigl;
9 trigl.Set(5, 6);
10 std::cout << "Rectangle(10, 20).Area() = " << rect.Area()
11 std::cout << "Triangle(5, 6).Area() = " << trigl.Area() <
12 return 0;

Click on the **Continue** button again and execution will stop at line number `11` of `dllmain.cpp` file.

Debugger is now debugging `libobject` project's source file, which is a separate project. If cursor is hovered `m_height` variable debugger will evaluate this variable and show its value.

It is evident that we can debug both DLL project and console app project at the same time. Larger projects can be debugged using a similar method. With this example we conclude our multiple app debugging session. Click on the **Stop** button to stop debugging.

Summary

In this chapter we learned app debugging with Code::Blocks using GNU GDB debugger. We learned various debugging related tools provided by Code::Blocks. Subsequently we learned debugging single and multiple apps.

In the next chapter we'll discuss app development for Windows.

4
Windows App Development with Code::Blocks

In the previous chapters, focus of our app development was on console based app. This is also known as text only app as console based apps can only display text and ASCII art. However, our focus in this chapter will be on app development for Windows.

Windows is one of the most widely used operating systems around the world. Code::Blocks can be used to develop apps for Windows, Linux, or Mac. Keeping in view the popularity of the Windows platform we shall restrict our focus to Windows platforms only.

Apps for Windows are also known as GUI (Graphical User Interface) based apps. User interaction with app is done by mouse and keyboard. Notepad app is an example of GUI based apps that come bundled with Windows operating system. The following screenshot displays the Notepad app:

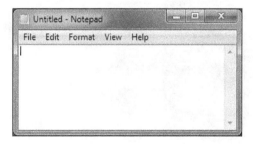

Code::Blocks comes along with all the tools required for Windows app development. Let's develop an app and learn it.

First Windows app

Following the tradition of Hello World app, we'll create our first Windows app. To do so perform the following steps:

1. Go to **File | New | Project...** menu option. Choose the **Win32 GUI project** option as in the following screenshot and click on the **Go** button:

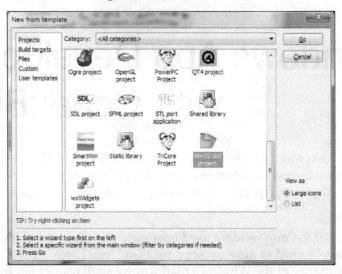

2. Click on the **Next** button on the first page of wizard as shown in the following screenshot. Choose **Frame based** option and click on the **Next** button. Dialog based apps can't contain menu bar or a toolbar. So we are choosing Frame based app.

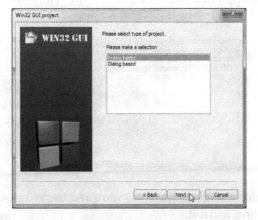

3. Enter App9 as project title and choose folder to create project. Now click on the **Next** button and then click on the **Finish** button to complete the wizard.

4. Replace code inside the `main.cpp` file with following code:

```
#include <windows.h>

int WINAPI WinMain(HINSTANCE thisInstance,
                   HINSTANCE prevInstance,
                   LPSTR     commandLine,
                   int       cmdShow
                   )
{
    MessageBox(NULL, "Hello World!", "Title", MB_OK | MB_
ICONINFORMATION);
    return 0;
}
```

5. Now click on the build icon in compiler toolbar. Click on the run button in compiler toolbar. Our `App9` window will be similar to the following screenshot:

6. Congratulations! We have successfully compiled our first app for Windows.

Let's understand the code we have written for this app. We are including `windows.h` file in the beginning of code. This file must be included in all Windows app as it contains relevant function declarations for Windows. Subsequently we have a function called `WinMain()` and this is the **entry point** of a Windows app. An entry point is the first function that is called at app start up.

The `WinMain()` functions accepts four parameters—handle to the current instance, handle to the previous instance, command line string pointer, and show state of window that controls how a app should be displayed.

We are calling the `MessageBox()` function to display a message box. It accepts four parameters—handle to the parent window (`NULL` or no one in our case), message text, dialog box title, and a combination of flags that controls buttons and icons to be shown. In our case we have used a combination of `MB_OK` and `MB_ICONINFORMATION`, which instructs the `MessageBox()` function to display a **OK** button and an information icon respectively.

But why are we getting a console for a GUI app? Answer is that by default Code::Blocks creates debug target as a console app. We can confirm this by navigating to **Project | Properties…** menu option and then clicking on the **Build targets** tab. Refer to the following screenshot:

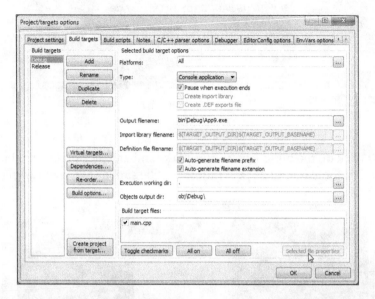

Advantage of this method is that debug output can be printed to that console for easier debugging. This can be disabled by changing app type to **GUI application** in the **Type:** combo box as shown in the following screenshot:

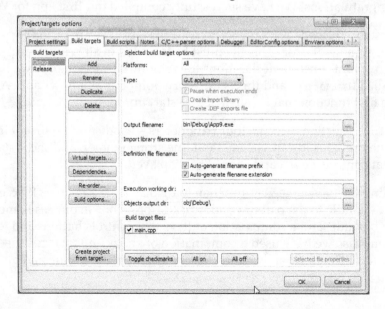

This will stop launching that console window.

Windows App and Unicode

Unicode is a standard to encode, store and represent text in World's most languages. C++ `char` data type is 1 byte in size. It is only able to represent text available in English language. To enable Unicode support in a Windows app we have to use a special data type called `wchar_t`, which is 2 byte in size. Let's say Hello World in the Hindi language. To do this we will replace previous `MessageBox()` code with the following code:

```
MessageBox(NULL, TEXT("हेलो वर्ल्ड"), TEXT("Title"), MB_OK | MB_
ICONINFORMATION);
```

The Code::Blocks editor window will look similar to the following screenshot. Editor font size has been changed to 16 point in order to work with Devnagiri script:

```
 2
 3    int WINAPI WinMain(HINSTANCE thisInstance,
 4                       HINSTANCE prevInstance,
 5                       LPSTR     commandLine,
 6                       int       cmdShow
 7                       )
 8    {
 9        MessageBox(NULL, TEXT("हेलो वर्ल्ड"), TEXT(
      "Title"), MB_OK | MB_ICONINFORMATION);
10        return 0;
11    }
12
```

We have decorated Hindi text with a `TEXT()` macro. This macro is used to translated a Unicode string to a `wchar_t*` when a `UNICODE` or `_UNICODE` pre-processor definition is defined. It returns a `char*` when Unicode support is not enabled.

Next we'll define following pre-processor defines. Go to **Project | Build options...** menu option. Then select App9 in the tree on the left side and click on the **Compiler settings** and then **#defines** tab.

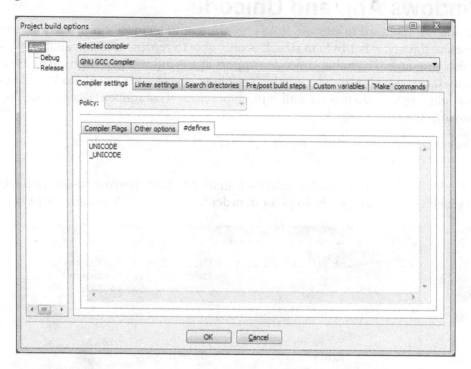

Add UNICODE and _UNICODE to the text control and click on the **OK** button. Click on the build button and then click on the run button in compiler toolbar. Now App9 will show Hello World in Hindi language, as shown in the following screenshot:

Please note that we'll enable Unicode support in all subsequent apps.

Event driven Windows app

Windows apps are **event driven** apps. An event can be an external or internal input to an app. Event driven apps run a message loop, which parses incoming events and then calls appropriate functions corresponding to that event. Code::Blocks default code generated by **Win32 GUI project** wizard generates a boilerplate code of an event driven app.

In order to understand event driven programming we shall be using following example to learn and understand it. We shall be using native Win32 API for this example. Win32 API is the base of several toolkits. Thus we should have an understanding of it in order to understand other toolkits.

Let's create another GUI app and name it App10. Replace wizard generated code with the following code. Also enable Unicode support as per the steps laid out in the previous example. As the code snippet is large we'll understand and paste it in editor window in several steps.

The following code snippet shows the header declaration, global variable declaration, and declaration of callback function:

```
#include <windows.h>
#define ID_BTN_CLICK_ME 100
// This function is called by the Windows function DispatchMessage()
LRESULT CALLBACK WindowProcedure (HWND hwnd, UINT message, WPARAM
wParam, LPARAM lParam);

// Make the class name into a global variable
TCHAR szClassName[ ] = TEXT("CodeBlocksWindowsApp");
```

In the following snippet we'll define the WinMain() function. We will define an object of WNDCLASSEX structure inside the WinMain() function. This structure takes several inputs. With wincl.lpfnWndProc we have assigned a callback function WindowProcedure() to the wincl object. This instructs app to call that function for event processing. Finally the wincl object will get registered with the RegisterClassEx() function. Once the object is registered successfully we create a window of that class using the CreateWindowEx() function.

We will display newly created window using the ShowWindow() function. After the window is displayed we will run an event processing loop using the GetMessage() function inside a while loop. All incoming events are then sent to the WindowProcedure() function by DispatchMessage() function.

```
int WINAPI WinMain (HINSTANCE hThisInstance,
                    HINSTANCE hPrevInstance,
                    LPSTR lpszArgument,
```

```
                      int nCmdShow)
{
    HWND hwnd;      // This is the handle for our window
    MSG messages; // Here messages to the application are saved
    WNDCLASSEX wincl; //Data structure for the windowclass

    // The Window structure
    wincl.hInstance = hThisInstance;
    wincl.lpszClassName = szClassName;
    wincl.lpfnWndProc = WindowProcedure;   // Callback function
    wincl.style = CS_DBLCLKS; // Catch double-clicks
    wincl.cbSize = sizeof (WNDCLASSEX);

    // Use default icon and mouse-pointer
    wincl.hIcon = LoadIcon (NULL, IDI_APPLICATION);
    wincl.hIconSm = LoadIcon (NULL, IDI_APPLICATION);
    wincl.hCursor = LoadCursor (NULL, IDC_ARROW);
    wincl.lpszMenuName = NULL;   /* No menu */
    wincl.cbClsExtra = 0;   // No extra bytes after the window class
    wincl.cbWndExtra = 0;   // structure or the window instance
    // Use Windows's default colour as the background of the window
    wincl.hbrBackground = (HBRUSH) COLOR_BACKGROUND;

    // Register the window class, and if it fails quit the program
    if (!RegisterClassEx (&wincl))
        return 0;

    // The class is registered, let's create the window
    hwnd = CreateWindowEx (
        0,              // Extended possibilites for variation
        szClassName,         // Classname
        TEXT("App for Windows"), // Title Text
        WS_OVERLAPPEDWINDOW, // default window
        CW_USEDEFAULT,   // Windows decides the position
        CW_USEDEFAULT,   // where the window ends up on the screen
        300,             // The programs width
        250,             // and height in pixels
        HWND_DESKTOP,    // The window is a child-window to desktop
        NULL,            // No menu
        hThisInstance,   // Program Instance handler
        NULL             // No Window Creation data
        );
```

```
    // Make the window visible on the screen
    ShowWindow (hwnd, nCmdShow);

    // Run the message loop. It will run until GetMessage() returns 0
    while (GetMessage (&messages, NULL, 0, 0))
    {
        // Translate virtual-key messages into character messages
        TranslateMessage(&messages);
        // Send message to WindowProcedure
        DispatchMessage(&messages);
    }

    // Return value of PostQuitMessage()
    return messages.wParam;
}
```

The WM_CREATE event is sent out by Windows OS when a window is being created. We will then create a button using the CreateWindow() function.

We shall be processing button press by processing the WM_COMMAND event in the WindowProcedure() function. We will then display a message box whenever this button is clicked.

Finally we will be processing the WM_DESTROY event, which will be issued whenever window is being destroyed. A return value of 0 will be posted with the PostQuitMessage() function emitting a WM_QUIT event to the message queue.

```
LRESULT CALLBACK WindowProcedure (HWND hwnd, UINT message, WPARAM
wParam, LPARAM lParam)
{switch (message) // handle the messages
    {
        case WM_CREATE:
            CreateWindow(TEXT("button"), TEXT("Click Me!"),
WS_VISIBLE | WS_CHILD, 20, 50, 80, 25, hwnd, (HMENU) ID_BTN_CLICK_ME,
NULL, NULL);
            break;
        case WM_COMMAND:
            if (LOWORD(wParam) == ID_BTN_CLICK_ME) {
                MessageBox(hwnd, TEXT("Hello World!"),
TEXT("Information"), MB_OK | MB_ICONINFORMATION);
            }
            break;
        case WM_DESTROY:
            PostQuitMessage (0); // send a WM_QUIT to the message
queue
```

```
            break;
        default:  // for messages that we don't deal with
            return DefWindowProc (hwnd, message, wParam, lParam);
    }

    return 0;
}
```

This completes our Windows app. Hit *F9* key (an alternative to clicking on the build and then run icon in build toolbar) to build and run this app. Following screenshot will be presented:

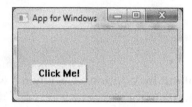

Advantages of Win32 API:

- Produces smaller executable size
- Produces faster code due to less overhead

Disadvantages of Win32 API:

- Requires longer development time due larger amount of code to be written
- Minimal set of GUI controls (for example, a text box, button, and so on) are available to developer

To solve this problem, GUI toolkit was developed. The GUI toolkit simplifies development process allowing reuse of code and a smaller code base. It also contains complex GUI control (for example, rich text control, HTML control, and so on).

wxWidgets GUI toolkit

A GUI toolkit is a set of header files and libraries that makes GUI development easier for developers. There are several GUI toolkits available in the market, few of them are stated as follows:

- **Microsoft Foundation Class (MFC)**: It is a set of classes that acts as a wrapper to Win32 api. This comes bundled with commercial versions of Visual Studio. MFC is proprietary and requires a Visual Studio license in order to use it. MFC app have native look and feel.

- **Qt** (pronounced as "cute"): It is a Open source and cross-platform GUI toolkit developed by **Digia**. Qt is licensed under both commercial and GPL/LGPL license. It is available on wide range of platforms including Windows, Linux, Mac, and so on. Qt drawn GUI is a custom drawn UI and may differ from a standard app on a platform.

- **wxWidgets**: It is another open source and cross-platform GUI toolkit licensed under wxWindows license (based on LGPL but less restrictive). It's generated UI has native look and feel as it uses platform standard UI elements.

We'll focus on wxWidgets toolkit in this book due to its simpler licensing model, native look and feel, and cross-platform development capability. A compiled copy of wxWidgets is also provided with the book. This book assumes that reader has extracted compiled wxWidgets to Z:\wxWidgets folder.

In order to understand similarities between Win32 API and wxWidgets we will recreate App9 functionalities with wxWidgets.

1. Go to **File | New | Project...** menu option. Then choose the **wxWidgets project** wizard.

2. Next click on the **Go** button and then click on the **Next** button in the next window. Choose **wxWidgets 2.9.x (SVN Version)** option in the wizard page and click on the **Next** button, as shown in the following screenshot:

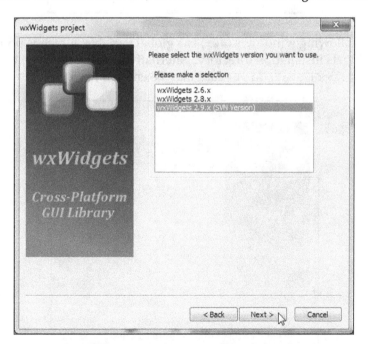

3. Enter `App11` as the Project title and click on the **Next** button. Click on the **Next** button to skip Project details page.

4. Choose **Frame Based** application type as shown in the following screenshot. Frame based apps are apps which can have menus, toolbars, and are suitable for large apps. Leave **Preferred GUI Builder** option to **None** as we'll be writing GUI code ourselves.

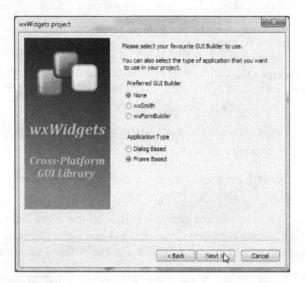

5. In the following window `$(#wx)` is a global variable, which is pointing to wxWidgets installation directory. Alternatively full path to wxWidgets that is `Z:\wxWidgets` in our case may be entered here:

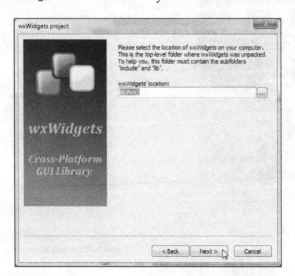

6. If this global variable is undefined at this point following window will pop up. It will not pop up if the global variable has already been defined.

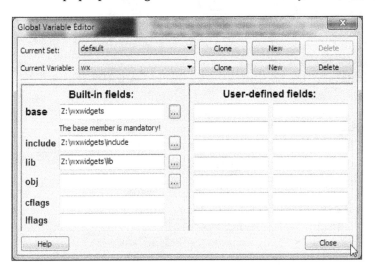

7. Complete the text boxes as per the previous screenshot and click on the **Close** button. Then click on the **Next** button twice.

8. Check the **Enable unicode** option in the following screenshot to enable Unicode support and click on the **Next** button. Click on the **Finish** button in the next page to close this wizard. Wizard will generate necessary code and set up a project to develop app using the wxWidgets toolkit.

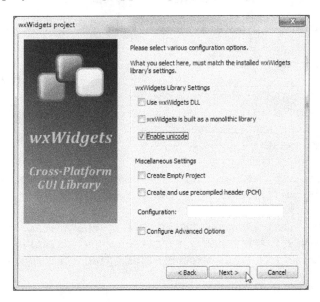

9. Replace code in the `App11Main.h` file with the following code:

```
#ifndef APP11MAIN_H
#define APP11MAIN_H

#include <wx/wx.h>
#include <wx/sizer.h>
#include <wx/button.h>

class App11Frame: public wxFrame {
    public:
        App11Frame(wxFrame *frame, const wxString& title);
        ~App11Frame();
    private:
        static const long idBtnClickMe;
        wxBoxSizer* m_boxSizerMain;
        wxButton* m_btnClickMe;
        void OnClickMe(wxCommandEvent& event);
        void OnClose(wxCloseEvent& event);
        DECLARE_EVENT_TABLE()
};
```

An `App11Frame` class has been derived from a `wxFrame` class. A `wxFrame` class represents a basic window. Member variable `m_btnClickMe` has been defined to create and store button and `idBtnClick` will store it's ID for event processing. We have placed a `DECLARE_EVENT_TABLE()` function macro to create boiler plate code for event handling related to this class.

10. Next replace code in the `App11Main.cpp` file with the following code:

```
#include "App11Main.h"
const long App11Frame::idBtnClickMe = ::wxNewId();

BEGIN_EVENT_TABLE(App11Frame, wxFrame)
    EVT_BUTTON(idBtnClickMe, App11Frame::OnClickMe)
    EVT_CLOSE(App11Frame::OnClose)
END_EVENT_TABLE()

App11Frame::App11Frame(wxFrame *frame, const wxString& title)
    : wxFrame(frame, -1, title)
{
    this->SetSizeHints(wxDefaultSize, wxDefaultSize);
    m_boxSizerMain = new wxBoxSizer(wxHORIZONTAL);
    m_btnClickMe = new wxButton(this, idBtnClickMe, _T("Click
Me!"),
```

```
                                      wxDefaultPosition, wxDefaultSize,
0);
    m_boxSizerMain->Add(m_btnClickMe, 0, wxALL, 5);
    this->SetSizer(m_boxSizerMain);
    this->Layout();
}

App11Frame::~App11Frame() {
}

void App11Frame::OnClose(wxCloseEvent &event) {
    Destroy();
}

void App11Frame::OnClickMe(wxCommandEvent& event) {
    wxMessageBox(_T("Hello World!"), _T("Information"), wxOK |
wxICON_INFORMATION, this);
}
```

An event table has been laid out using BEGIN_EVENT_TABLE() and END_EVENT_TABLE() macros. This defines relationship of callback functions with respective events. The OnClickMe() function has been connected to button press event. It will show a message whenever the **Click Me!** button is pressed by the user.

The OnClose() function will be called when app closed. It calls a Destroy() function that initiates app shutdown.

11. Now replace code in the App11App.h file with the following code:

```
#ifndef APP11APP_H
#define APP11APP_H

#include <wx/app.h>

class App11App : public wxApp
{
    public:
        virtual bool OnInit();
};

#endif // APP11APP_H
```

In the preceding file we have derived a class App11App from wxApp. A virtual function OnInit() is implemented in this class.

12. Next type the following code in the `App11App.cpp` file:

```
#include "App11App.h"
#include "App11Main.h"

IMPLEMENT_APP(App11App);

bool App11App::OnInit() {
    App11Frame* frame = new App11Frame(0L, _("wxWidgets
Application Template"));
    #ifdef __WXMSW__
    frame->SetIcon(wxICON(aaaa)); // To Set App Icon
    #endif
    frame->Show();

    return true;
}
```

In the implementation of `OnInit()` function an object named `frame` has been derived from the `App11Frame` class. Resource files are available only on Windows platform. Thus it has been enclosed within a pre-processor macro `__WXMSW__` and subsequently app is launched in line number 12.

13. Leave code inside `resource.rc` file as it is.

14. Hit *F9* button to compile and run. Following window will be launched. We find that our application is now working fine:

Earlier we mentioned about cross-platform development capability of wxWidgets. Let's put that capability into action. We'll compile `App11` source without any change on Linux platform. For this example, we are using **CentOS 6** Linux.

In order to compile on Linux platform, we'll use a `Makefile`. Remember we can also use the Code::Blocks wxWidgets project wizard to generate a project targeted at Linux platform. However in my opinion developers should be familiar with the `Make` tool.

Make is a build tool that can be used any number of source files to a binary based files on a set of rules inside a text file known as a `Makefile`. Make handles build dependencies efficiently and for a large project make will only compile relevant files, which has changed since last build. This saves time and also eliminates any human error in the entire build process.

Perform the following steps:

1. Paste the following code into a file and save it with filename `Makefile`:

```
CPP=g++
CXXFLAGS=-c $(shell wx-config --cflags)
LDFLAGS=$(shell wx-config --libs)
SOURCES=App11Main.cpp App11App.cpp

App11: App11Main.o App11App.o
    $(CPP) $(LDFLAGS) App11Main.o App11App.o -o App11

App11Main.o:
    $(CPP) $(CXXFLAGS) App11Main.cpp

App11App.o:
    $(CPP) $(CXXFLAGS) App11App.cpp

clean:
    rm -rf *.o App11
```

In this file several variables are defined in first four lines. The CPP variable defines C++ compiler binary, CXXFLAGS stores necessary compiler flags for a wxWidgets project by running a script wx-config. The wxWidgets project provides a shell script known as wx-config that can be used determine compiler and linker flags.

LDFLAGS stores necessary linker flags used for executable binary generation. SOURCES variable define the sources that are to be compiled. Do note that we are not using resource.rc file anymore as resource compiler doesn't exist on Linux platform.

App11: line defines a make target App11 which comprises two sub-targets App11Main.o and App11App.o. There is a shell command defined in the following line which indicates the command to be executed after all sub-targets are built successfully. Subsequently both these targets are also defined in a similar manner.

clean: target executes a command to delete all object files and our executable binary.

2. Next issue the following command in Linux shell prompt to compile our app:

   ```
   [biplab@centos App11]$ make
   ```

3. To run our app use the following command:

   ```
   [biplab@centos App11]$ ./App11
   ```

4. Following window will be displayed:

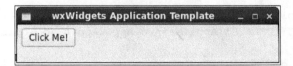

We find that our app now runs on Linux platform flawlessly. It behaves exactly as we wanted it to. We didn't make any changes to the code we wrote for Windows platform. But our GUI toolkit has internally mapped our code to appropriate functions for Linux platform. This gives an immense advantage to a developer as targeting multiple platforms becomes a lot easier.

Rapid app development with wxSmith

We have learned about app development for Windows platform in the last few sections. But all our code was hand-written. We also noticed that even for a simple GUI we have to write several lines of code.

So, can we do something about it? How about automatic code generation of GUI codes? Sound interesting! Code::Blocks comes with a plugin, called **wxSmith**, which can generate C++ code (using wxWidgets toolkit) based on the user generated GUI inside a Visual editor. We'll learn this with another example.

1. Create a new wxWidgets project. This time we'll name it something meaningful. In the following window enter project title as MyNotePad.

2. In the following page, select **wxSmith** as **Preferred GUI Builder**. This option configures wxWidgets project to use wxSmith GUI builder. Refer the following screenshot:

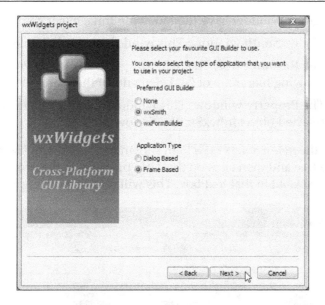

3. After the project generation is complete files following window will be displayed:

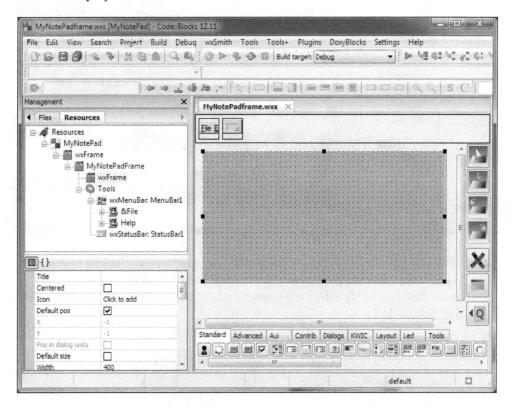

4. The preceding window have the following three major components:

    ° The **wxSmith** window: This window shows editable UI elements

    ° The **Resource** tree: This window gives an overall view of the project showing hierarchy of GUI elements of that particular project

    ° The **Property** window: This window shows properties of currently selected object in wxSmith window

5. Click on the `MyNotePadFrame` item shown in the following screenshot on the resource tree and then click on the **Title** property in the property window. Type `MyNotePad` in that text box. This will set title of our app to `MyNotePad`.

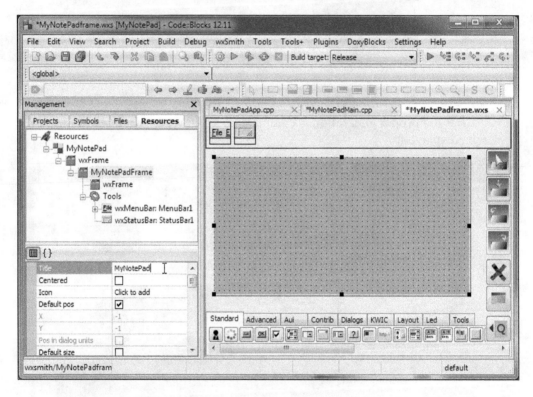

6. Now we'll add a `wxTextCtrl` control to our app. This will add a text box to our app. Click on the `wxTextCtrl` control button on the toolbar below. Immediately the **MyNotePadFrame** window shown inside wxSmith window will be selected.

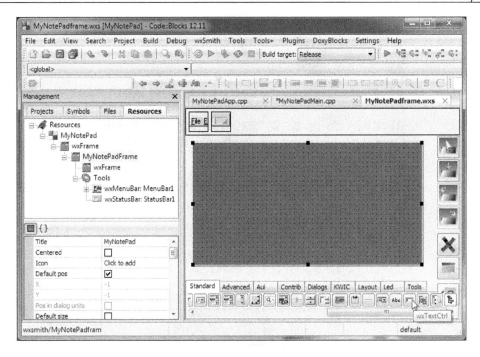

7. Click on it and this text control will be added to that. The wxSmith window will look similar to the following screenshot:

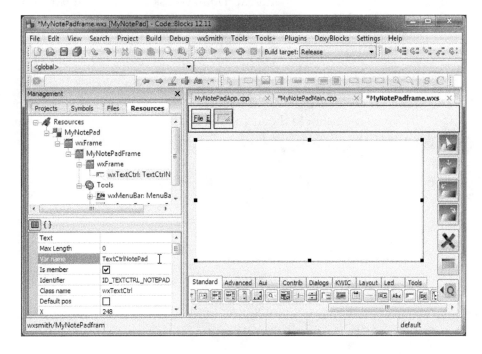

8. In the property window change the following properties:

    ° **Text** property: It is an empty string. This property stores the text inside a text control

    ° **Var name** property: Change this to `TextCtrlNotePad`. This property will be used to name object of the `wxTextCtrl` class.

    ° **Identifier** property `ID_TEXTCTRL_NOTEPAD`: It will be assigned a unique integer and then will be used to assign it with an event handler and an event type.

9. Scroll down the property window and click on the **Style** property. Click on the **wxTE_MULTILINE** property to check it. This will enable text control show text in multiple lines.

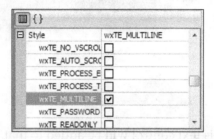

10. In this next step, we'll edit menu bar. Double-click on the menu bar icon (shown in following screenshot):

11. The **MenuBar editor** window will pop up. Select the **Quit** menu option as in the following screenshot in the menu tree on the left side and then click on the **New** button:

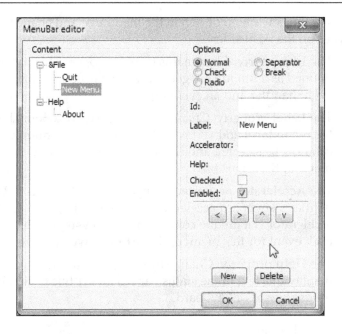

12. Click on the ^ button to move the new menu item above, **Quit** menu option. Four buttons shown in the following screenshot can be used to rearrange menu items in the menu tree:

13. Now select the new menu option in the menu tree and change the following properties on the right side:

   ° The **Id** property: Change this to `idFileOpen`. This property will be defined as a unique integer and will be used to assign it with an event handler and an event type.

   ° The **Label** property: Change this property to `&Open`. This text defines the menu label and `&O` text will define an accelerator key. This menu can now be selected and clicked by pressing *O* button whenever this menu option is visible.

   ° The **Accelerator** property: Change this one to `Ctrl+O`. This property defines a keyboard accelerator to this menu option. A keyboard accelerator is a unique combination of keystrokes that will generate a click event for this menu option irrespective of menu item's visibility.

   ° The **Help** property: Change this to `Opens a file...` text. This will display this text in the status bar whenever this option is selected by mouse cursor or keyboard.

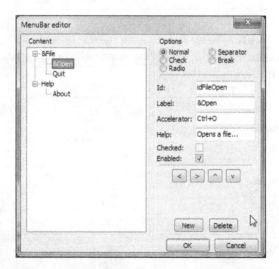

14. Click on the **OK** button to close this window. We have now added a menu option to our existing menu bar. Before we add code to open a file with this menu option we need to add a file open save control.

15. Click on the **Dialogs** tab and then click on the **wxFileDialog** control button. This will add a standard file open and save dialog to the `MyNotePadFrame` class.

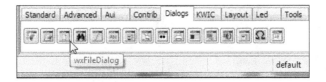

16. Change the following properties in property window:

    ° **Wildcard** to `*.txt`. This will set the filter text to files with `.txt` extension.

    ° **Var name** to `NotePadFileDialog`. This will be used to create an object of the `wxFileDialog` class that represents a standard open or save dialog.

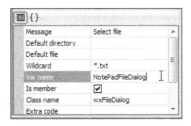

17. Now we are set to add code to newly added menu option. Click on the **&Open** item in the resource tree and then click on the {} button in property window. Click on the dropdown box and choose the **-- Add new handler --** menu option as in the following screenshot:

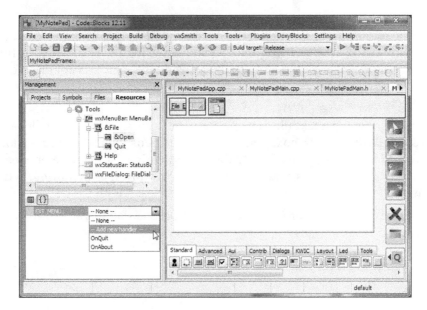

18. Enter `OnFileOpen` text in the dialog box and then click on the **OK** button, as shown in the following screenshot:

19. Code editor window will be open. Add the following code to the `MyNotePadFrame::OnFileOpen()` function.

```
int result;
wxTextFile textFile;
wxString fileContent;

result = NotePadFileDialog->ShowModal();
if (result == wxID_OK) {
   if (textFile.Open(NotePadFileDialog->GetPath())) {
      for (size_t i = 0; i < textFile.GetLineCount(); i++) {
         fileContent << textFile.GetLine(i) << _T("\r\n");
      }
      textFile.Close();
      TextCtrlNotePad->SetLabel(fileContent);
   }
}
```

Let's explain preceding code. We have defined couple of variables in the beginning. We are showing file open dialog using the `ShowModal()` function and result of this dialog will be stored inside the `result` variable. Next line checks that we have received a `wxID_OK` value, which indicates that user has selected a file.

We are opening a text file in using the `Open()` function with the filename received from dialog box. If file opening succeeds then we'll create a loop to read all lines one by one. The `fileContent` variable appends a line read from file and then appends a new line (`\r\n` on Windows) to this string. When we are done reading all lines opened text file is closed with the `Close()` function.

Finally we set text stored inside `fileContent` variable is stored to our main text control.

We also need to include an extra header file in order to use the `wxTextFile` class. Add the following line after the `#include <wx/msgdlg.h>` line in the `MyNotePadMain.cpp` file:

```
#include <wx/textfile.h>
```

20. We are now ready to compile our little notepad app. Hit *F9* key to build and run it. Our app will look similar to the following screenshot:

21. Go to **File** | **Open** menu option and following dialog box will be opened:

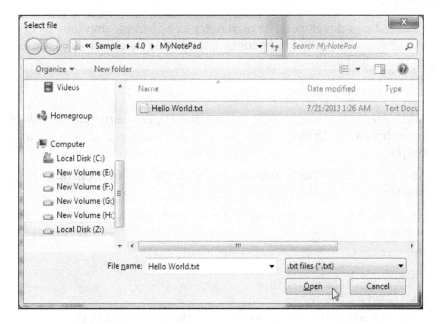

22. Click on the **Open** button and the selected text file will now be opened by our app, as shown in the following screenshot:

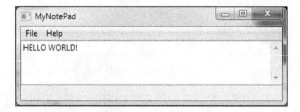

Our app is now working! We wrote most of our GUI related code with the help of Code::Blocks. Only code that was manually written was the one we have inserted to open a text file. Code::Blocks offers an excellent cross-platform and rapid application development platform. We can develop a GUI app with Code::Blocks easily using this approach.

Exercise

We have learned and developed our own notepad app in the previous section. However, our app was limited to opening a file. In this exercise we will extend our app to save a text file.

We'll perform the following steps:

1. Add a menu item &Save to file menu after &Open menu option, with Ctrl+S as keyboard accelerator, idFileSave as ID and Saves a file... as Help text.

2. Add an event handler to this menu option and add event handler function OnFileSave().

3. Finally add the following code to the MyNotePadFrame::OnFileSave() function:

```
int result;

result = NotePadFileDialog->ShowModal();
if (result == wxID_OK) {
  if (!TextCtrlNotePad->SaveFile(NotePadFileDialog-
    >GetPath())) {
    wxMessageBox(_T("Couldn't save ") + NotePadFileDialog-
      >GetPath(),
        _T("Error"), wxOK | wxICON_ERROR);
  }
}
```

This code is similar to the code we wrote for the `OnFileOpen()` function. We are using the `wxTextCtrl::FileSave()` function to save our file in line number 5. Code in line number 6 ensures that an error message should be shown when a file can't be written.

I leave it to you to follow earlier steps and complete this exercise. You can refer accompanying MyNotePad app source code for this completed exercise.

Summary

In this chapter we have learned app development for Windows using Win32 api and Code::Blocks. We then focused on GUI toolkit and developed our first app for Windows and Linux using wxWidgets toolkit.

Code::Blocks also has a rapid application development toolkit and we used it to develop our own Notepad app.

In the next chapter we'll take one app and learn how to plan and develop it from scratch.

5
Programming Assignment

We have learned about Code:Blocks and app development for Windows in previous chapters. In this chapter we will use this knowledge and develop an app from scratch as an exercise. We will first take a look at the final app and then develop it from ground up. We will use the tools we learned in the previous chapters, which you can refer as you need.

Developing MyPaint – an image viewer

We will develop an image viewer app as an exercise in this chapter. Our image viewer app shall have the following features:

- It shall open `.jpeg`, `.png`, and `.bmp` files
- It shall allow user to zoom in and out of the loaded image at an interval of 10 percent
- Zoom range shall be within 10 percent to 200 percent
- There shall be keyboard shortcuts assigned to most commands
- There shall be toolbar to provide access to commonly used functions
- The app shall be developed using wxSmith plugin of Code::Blocks
- The app shall use wxWidgets toolkit

Our app shall look like the following screenshot. The following screenshot shows our image viewer app has opened the Koala.jpg file (part of Windows 7 standard wallpaper set) with a zoom level set at 60 percent.

Looks interesting, doesn't it? Let us begin our exercise and solve it. We'll do it in two steps.

1. Understand the structure of our image viewer app.
2. Begin app development with Code::Blocks.

Anatomy of exercise app

Our image viewer app uses several C++ classes to open, display, and control display of image. The following screenshot highlights major classes that are responsible for user interaction:

Let us see more about the classes listed in the following bullet list:

- The wxFrame class: This class represents main window. All other visual elements are displayed inside this class.

- The wxMenuBar class: This class shows the menu bar in our app.

- The wxToolBar class: This class shows a tool bar in our app.

- The wxScrolledWindow class: This class is used to display images. This class creates a resizable window to match window size.

- The wxStatusBar class: This class shows a status bar at the bottom of our app. We'll be using this to display menu item help and other information.

A tree of the classes and their relationship with the `wxFrame` derived class is shown in the following diagram:

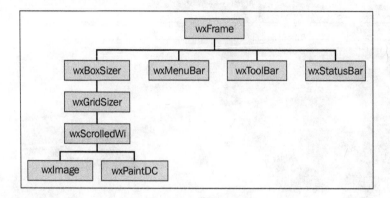

In the preceding diagram `wxMenuBar`, `wxToolBar`, and `wxStatusBar` are derived classes and have been added directly to `wxFrame` derived class.

Whereas we need couple of extra classes for the `wxScrolledWindow` derived class. We have two intermediate classes, `wxBoxSizer` and `wxGridSizer`, for the `wxScrolledWindow` derived class. These classes are known as layout classes that help laying out child windows within a parent window. Note that layout classes are not visible to the user.

wxWidgets provides a class to load, manipulate multiple image formats via the `wxImage` class. This class is the engine of our app. The `wxScrolledWindow` class uses it to load and manipulate image file. `wxPaintDC` is the class that `wxScrolledWindow` uses to paint loaded image file on to itself.

With this introduction to the structure of our app we shall proceed with the development of our app.

Solution of exercise problem

Let us solve it step-by-step by performing the following steps:

1. Create a new `wxWidgets` project and set the project name to `MyPaint`. Choose **wxSmith** as the **Preferred GUI Builder**.

2. Click on the **wxFrame** in the **Management** pane as shown in the following screenshot:

3. Set the `Title` property to `MyPaint`.

4. Click on the **Layout** tab and click on the wxBoxSizer button as shown in the following screenshot. Then click on the frame shown inside wxSmith window:

5. Next add a wxGridSizer to the newly added wxBoxSizer in a similar manner. Refer to the following screenshot for the wxGridSizer button. After wxGridSizer is added set the **Cols** property to 1.

6. Click on the **Standard** tab and add a wxScrolledWindow to the wxGridSizer as per the following screenshot:

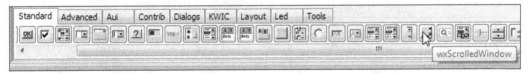

7. Set the following properties for wxScrolledWindow:
   - **Var name** to `MyPaintWindow`
   - **Min Width** to `640` and **Min Height** to `480`
   - **Border Width** to 5.

8. At this step the **Management** pane shall look similar to the following screenshot:

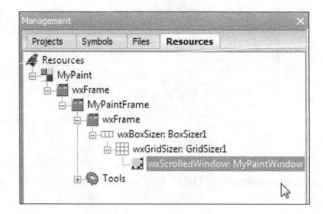

9. Click on the **Dialogs** tab and click on the wxFileDialog button. Set the following properties according to the bullet list:

   ° **Message** to Select file

   ° **Wildcard** to *.bmp;*.jpg;*.png

   ° **Var name** to MyPaintFileDialog

10. Click on the **Tools** in the **Management** pane can click on the wxStatusBar item. Set the following properties:

   ° **Var name** to StatusBarMain

   ° **Fields** to 2

   ° In **Field 1**, **Width** to 5

   ° In **Field 2**, **Width** to 10.

11. Next open the **MenuBar Editor** and add menu items as per the next screenshot:

Menu item	ID	Label	Accelerator	Help item
&File | &Open Image	idFileOpen	&Open Image	Ctrl + O	Opens an Image file...
&View | Zoom &In	idViewZoomIn	Zoom &In	Ctrl++	Zooms +10%
&View | Zoom &Out	idViewZoomOut	Zoom &Out	Ctrl+-	Zooms -10%

The final menu bar editor window shall look similar to the following screenshot:

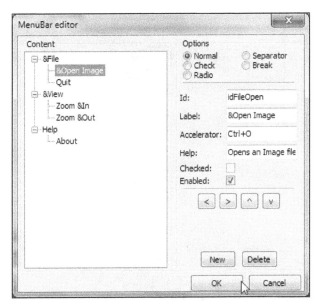

12. We'll now add a wxToolBar to our app. Click on the **Tools** tab as shown in the following screenshot and click on the wxToolBar button to add a wxToolBar to our app.

13. Double-click on the wxToolBar icon in the wxSmith window and add the following items.

Label	Options	Bitmap	Tooltip/Help text
Open an image...	Normal	Image from wxArtProvider – wxART_FILE_OPEN	Opens an image file
–	Separator	–	–
Zoom in	Normal	zoom_in.png file from the project folder	Zoom in by 10%
Zoom out	Normal	zoom_out.png file from the project folder	Zoom out by 10%

The final **ToolBar editor** window will look similar to the following screenshot.

We have completed addition of most GUI elements. We need to write code to complete our app. Before doing that please note that wxSmith generated code remains inside the matching //(* and //*) block. Do not write your code inside this block as wxSmith will delete any custom code within this block while regenerating code.

14. Add the following code inside the MyPaintFrame class declaration in the MyPaintFrame.h file as a private member variable and function.

```
wxImage* m_Image; //  To store loaded image
double m_zoomFactor; // To store current zoom factor
void RefreshPaintWindow(void); // To paint image
```

15. Add the following code inside the MyPaintFrame() constructor function. We will be creating a new image class and assign it to m_Image variable. We'll use SetScrollbars() and ShowScrollbars() function to assign scroll bar related properties. We'll assign initial zoom factor of 100 percent and use the wxInitAllImageHandlers() function to initialize image processing engine for our app. Finally we'll use the SetStatusText() function to set status bar text.

```
m_Image = new wxImage(640, 480);
MyPaintWindow->SetScrollbars(10, 10, 10, 10);
MyPaintWindow->ShowScrollbars(wxSHOW_SB_ALWAYS, wxSHOW_SB_
ALWAYS);
m_zoomFactor = 1.0;
```

```
wxInitAllImageHandlers();
StatusBarMain->SetStatusText(_T("Ready!"), 0);
wxString msg;
msg.Printf(_T("%d %%"), static_cast<int>(m_zoomFactor*100));
StatusBarMain->SetStatusText(msg, 1);
```

16. Click on the resources tree and navigate to **&File | &Open Image** menu option. Go to the **Events** tab (identified by {}), click on the dropdown menu next to **EVT_MENU** and select the **--- Add new handler ---** menu option. Enter OnFileOpen as the name of the event handler. Then enter the following code inside the MyPaintFrame::OnFileOpen() function:

```
int result;

result = MyPaintFileDialog->ShowModal();
if (result == wxID_OK) {
    m_Image->LoadFile(MyPaintFileDialog->GetPath());
    m_zoomFactor = 1.0;
    RefreshPaintWindow();
}
```

17. Next add the OnViewZoomIn and OnViewZoomOut event handler function to **Zoom &In** and **Zoom &Out** by navigating to **&View | Zoom &In** and **&View | Zoom &Out** menu options respectively. Refer completed exercise for the code to be added to each handler.

18. Select **MyPaintWindow** from the resources tree and click on the **Events** tab. Add the OnMyPaintWindowPaint event handler to **EVT_PAINT** and paste the following code. This code paints loaded image on wxScrolledWindow:

```
wxPaintDC paintDC(MyPaintWindow);
wxRect rect;
const wxBitmap bitmap(m_Image->Scale(m_Image->GetWidth() * m_
zoomFactor,
                                     m_Image->GetHeight() * m_
zoomFactor));

rect.SetSize(m_Image->GetSize() * m_zoomFactor);
MyPaintWindow->SetVirtualSize(m_Image->GetSize() * m_
zoomFactor);

if ( (rect.GetWidth() < MyPaintWindow->GetVirtualSize().
GetWidth()) ||
```

```
        (rect.GetHeight() < MyPaintWindow->GetVirtualSize().
GetHeight()) ) {
        rect = rect.CenterIn(MyPaintWindow->GetVirtualSize());
}

MyPaintWindow->DoPrepareDC(paintDC);
paintDC.DrawBitmap(bitmap, rect.GetTopLeft());
```

19. Add `OnResize` event handler to **MyPaintWindow** and add the following line of code:

    ```
    RefreshPaintWindow();
    ```

20. Next add `RefreshPaintWindow()` function to the `MyPaintFrame` class and add the following code inside that function:

    ```
    wxString msg;

    MyPaintWindow->ClearBackground();
    MyPaintWindow->Refresh();
    msg.Printf(_T("%d %%"), static_cast<int>(m_zoomFactor*100));
    StatusBarMain->SetStatusText(msg, 1);
    ```

21. Now we'll add code to our toolbar buttons. Select the **Item: Open an image...** item in the resource tree and go to the **Events** tab. Add the existing `OnFileOpen` event handler to **EVT_TOOL**. This will connect the existing `OnFileOpen()` function to this toolbar button. So clicking on this toolbar button will emulate navigating to the **File | Open menu** options.

22. Follow previous steps and connect the **Zoom in** and **Zoom out** toolbar buttons to `OnViewZoomIn` and `OnViewZoomOut` event handlers respectively.

23. Our app is now complete. Hit *F9* key to build and run. Upon successful build app will be run and we'll be presented with app window. Now open any image file and enjoy viewing it inside your freshly written app. Our app will now look as per the following screenshot:

Summary

We planned and wrote our own image viewer app in this exercise. We have used the RAD capability of Code::Blocks to write our app and we found that we can write an app from scratch within a short period of time.

With this we conclude our book on app development with C++ and Code::Blocks. C++ is a vast subject. Code::Blocks also has numerous features. It is impossible to highlight each and every aspect of them. I hope that with this book I have been able to shed light on app development with C++ and Code::Blocks. I also believe this book has also shown that app development with C++ and Code::Blocks can be fun and exciting.

Appendix

This Appendix focuses on the feature set of Code::Blocks. Apart from code editing, managing, and building, Code::Blocks has numerous other features. It can be scripted to extend features of Code::Blocks. It has plugin to generate documentation of code. It is also able to export code in different formats such as rich text format, portable document format, and so on. It can also manage snippets of code to ease the development process. We shall discuss about them in the next couple of sections.

Scripting Code::Blocks

Code::Blocks uses **Squirrel** language for scripting. Squirrel language is a high-level, object oriented, and light weight programming language. Squirrel syntax is similar to C/C++ programing language.

Code::Blocks exposes a large amount of its API via scripting. As a result several aspects of Code::Blocks can be extended via scripting.

Refer to the documentation from the following URLS for scripting references:

- **Scripting commands**: http://wiki.codeblocks.org/index.php?title=Scripting_commands
- **API bindings**: http://wiki.codeblocks.org/index.php?title=Script_bindings

Documentation generation

Documentation of code is very important for any project. It builds an overview of the written code, explains its usage, and helps developers understand the code. Code::Blocks allows generation of code documentation from the IDE itself.

Doxygen is a standard tool to create documentation from annotated C++ files. Code::Blocks comes with a plugin called **DoxyBlocks** that creates an interface with the externally installed doxygen tool.

We need to download and install doxygen tool first. Subsequently we can use DoxyBlocks plugin to generate documentation. Perform the following steps:

1. Download doxygen from the following URL – `http://www.stack.nl/~dimitri/doxygen/download.html`. Also download `doxygen-x.x.x-setup.exe` file. Double-click on that file to install it.

2. We need to connect DoxyBlocks plugin with doxygen tool. Go to **DoxyBlocks | Open preferences…** menu option. The following screenshot will be displayed:

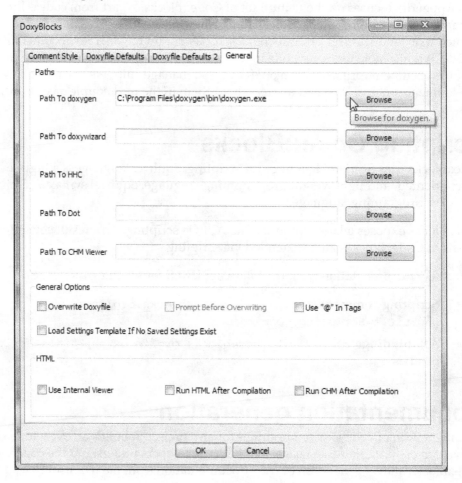

3. Click on the **General** tab. Next click on the **Browse** button next to **Path To doxygen** option and set the path to `C:\Program Files\doxygen\bin\doxygen.exe`.

4. Next create a new C++ console project and add the following code to wizard generated `main.cpp` file:

```cpp
class A {
    public:
        A() {};
        ~A() {};
        virtual int CallMe(int a) = 0;
};

class B : public A {
    public:
        B() {};
        ~B() {};
        int CallMe(int a) {
            return a;
        }
};

int main() {
    return 0;
}
```

5. Navigate to **DoxyBlocks | Extract documentation** menu option or press *Ctrl + Alt+ E* key combination. Code::Blocks will now generate documentation of the project inside `doxygen` folder.

6. Go to **DoxyBlocks | Run HTML** menu option or press the *Ctrl + Alt + H* key combination to open the newly created documentation in a Web browser.

    We can also add additional detailed description of function, class, etc to create a detailed documentation.

7. Move the cursor to the beginning of `B::CallMe()` function and click on the **DoxyBlocks | /** Block comment** menu option or press *Ctrl + Alt + B* key combination. Code::Blocks will analyze the function parameters and will insert a default comment block suitable for doxygen tool. Adjust the comment block and our code will look similar to the following snippet:

```cpp
        ~B() {};
        /** \brief Virtual function CallMe() is defined here
         *
         * \param a int
```

```
 * \return int
 *
 */
int CallMe(int a) {
```

8. Press *Ctrl + Alt + E* key combination to regenerate the documentation and use the *Ctrl + Alt + H* key combination to open it inside Web browser. Documentation of `B::CallMe()` will look similar to the following screenshot:

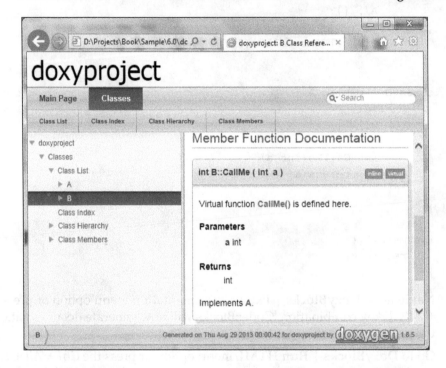

We can also customize DoxyBlocks plugin option to use advanced features of doxygen.

Management of code snippets

Code::Blocks allows developers to store and retrieve frequently used code snippets. We have used DoxyBlocks plugin in our previous example to comment blocks suitable for generating documents. However we can also save a blank template as a code snippet and reuse it wherever needed.

1. Go to **View | Code snippets** menu option to show the **CodeSnippets** window.

2. Right-click on the `codesnippets` in the tree and select **Add SubCategory** menu option.

3. Name it `doxygen`. Right-click on this **doxygen** category and click on the **Add snippet** menu option.

4. Enter `Block comment` as **Label** and following code as the snippet text:

```
\** \brief
   *
   */
```

5. Click on the **OK** button to save this snippet. **CodeSnippets** window will look similar to the following screenshot:

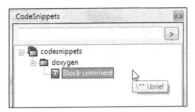

6. Now click on any place in the Code::Blocks editor window, right-click on this snippet and select **Apply** menu option. This snippet will now be pasted into the Editor window.

We can add code, bookmarks, text files as a code snippet. Code snippets are not project specific and works across all the projects.

Use of external tools for a project

Code::Blocks allows user to use external tools for any project. Imagine we want to use doxygen tool to generate documentation without using the DoxyBlocks plugin. We can add doxygen as an external tool and then use it on demand.

1. Go to **Tools | Configure tools...** menu option to add a new tool. The following window will be opened:

2. Click on the **Add** button to add a new tool. The following window will be opened:

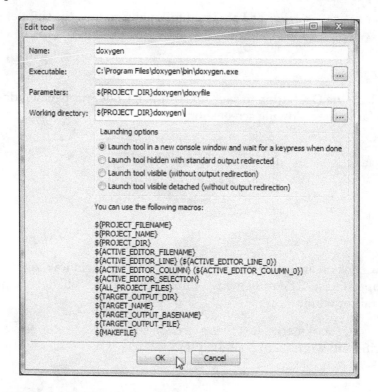

3. Enter following details:

    °   Set **Name** property to doxygen. This value will be used to create a new menu item under **Tools** menu

    °   Set **Executable** property to C:\Program Files\doxygen\bin\doxygen.exe

    °   Set **Parameters** property to ${PROJECT_DIR}doxygen\doxyfile

    °   Set **Working** directory property to ${PROJECT_DIR}doxygen\

4. Click on the **OK** button to close this window and then click on the **OK** button to close **User-defined tools** window. A menu item will be created under **Tools** menu option.

5. Navigate to **Tools | doxygen** menu option and the doxygen tool will be launched inside a console window. Press any key to close this console window when it has completed.

We can use any other tool in a similar manner.

Exporting source code in different format

Code::Blocks allows user to export source code to HTML, RTF, ODF, or PDF format. Perform the following steps to export source in different format:

1. To export a file as PDF format go to **File | Export | As PDF...** menu option.

2. Enter a file name and path in the next dialog. Click on the **Save** button to continue.

3. Code::Block will prompt to confirm inclusion of line numbers in the exported source code. Select **Yes** or **No** option and that particular source file will be exported.

Index

Thank you for buying
C++ Application Development with Code::Blocks

About Packt Publishing

Packt, pronounced 'packed', published its first book "*Mastering phpMyAdmin for Effective MySQL Management*" in April 2004 and subsequently continued to specialize in publishing highly focused books on specific technologies and solutions.

Our books and publications share the experiences of your fellow IT professionals in adapting and customizing today's systems, applications, and frameworks. Our solution based books give you the knowledge and power to customize the software and technologies you're using to get the job done. Packt books are more specific and less general than the IT books you have seen in the past. Our unique business model allows us to bring you more focused information, giving you more of what you need to know, and less of what you don't.

Packt is a modern, yet unique publishing company, which focuses on producing quality, cutting-edge books for communities of developers, administrators, and newbies alike. For more information, please visit our website: www.packtpub.com.

About Packt Open Source

In 2010, Packt launched two new brands, Packt Open Source and Packt Enterprise, in order to continue its focus on specialization. This book is part of the Packt Open Source brand, home to books published on software built around Open Source licences, and offering information to anybody from advanced developers to budding web designers. The Open Source brand also runs Packt's Open Source Royalty Scheme, by which Packt gives a royalty to each Open Source project about whose software a book is sold.

Writing for Packt

We welcome all inquiries from people who are interested in authoring. Book proposals should be sent to author@packtpub.com. If your book idea is still at an early stage and you would like to discuss it first before writing a formal book proposal, contact us; one of our commissioning editors will get in touch with you.

We're not just looking for published authors; if you have strong technical skills but no writing experience, our experienced editors can help you develop a writing career, or simply get some additional reward for your expertise.

Microsoft Visual C++ Windows Applications by Example

ISBN: 978-1-847195-56-2   Paperback: 440 pages

Code and explanation for real-world MFC C++ Applications

1. Learn C++ Windows programming by studying realistic, interesting examples

2. A quick primer in Visual C++ for programmers of other languages, followed by deep, thorough examples

3. Example applications include a Tetris-style game, a spreadsheet application, a drawing application, and a word processor

Boost C++ Application Development Cookbook

ISBN: 978-1-849514-88-0   Paperback: 348 pages

Over 80 practical, task-based recipes to create applications using Boost libraries

1. Explores how to write a program once and then use it on Linux, Windows, MacOS, and Android operating systems

2. Includes everyday use recipes for multithreading, networking, metaprogramming, and generic programming from a Boost library developer

4. Take advantage of the real power of Boost and C++ to get a good grounding in using it in any project

Please check **www.PacktPub.com** for information on our titles